THE HISTORY OF THE
WESTERN RAILROADS

THE HISTORY OF THE
WESTERN
RAILROADS

JANE ELIOT

Crescent Books
New York/Avenel, New Jersey

This 1995 edition published by Crescent Books,
distributed by Random House Value Publishing, Inc.,
40 Engelhard Avenue,
Avenel, New Jersey 07001.

Random House
New York Toronto London Sydney Auckland

Produced by Brompton Books Corporation,
15 Sherwood Place,
Greenwich, Connecticut 06830

ISBN 0-517-12170-0

8 7 6 5 4 3 2 1

Printed and bound in China

Editing by Barbara A. Paulding and Bill Yenne
Design by Bill Yenne
Captions by Susan Garratt and Bill Yenne
Picture research by Rod Baird, Bill Yenne and John Crowley

PICTURE CREDITS

AGS Archives 135
Alaska Railroad 106 (both), 107 (top)
Association of American Railroads 7, 23, 64
Baltimore & Ohio Railroad Company 8-9, 12, 13
The Bancroft Library, University of California, Berkeley 26, 27 (top), 39, 45,47, 56, 60-6l, 84-85(bottom)
Bison Picture Library 10-11, 50-5l, 54, 55
Burlington Northern Railroad 2-3, 20-2l, 24-25, 48, 65(top), 94-95, 108, 112, 113(top), 117, 130-31, 140-41, 142(bottom), 144 (both), 150-51, 179
Canadian National 99 (both), 100-01, 102, 102-03, 136 (top 2), 136-37, (all 3), 182-83
Canadian Pacific Rail 95, 122, 136 (bottom 2)
Chicago & Eastern Illinois Railroad 18-19
Al Chione 177 (top), 178-79, 180-81
Delaware & Hudson Railroad Company 7
Denver & Rio Grande Western Railroad 86-87
Globe Photos 176
© DW Golde 2-3, 4-5, 154-173
Gulf Oil Company 1l5
Nashville, Chattanooga & St Louis Railway 21
National Railway Historical Society 40-41, 56-57, 69, 70-71, 74
Pennsylvania Railroad Company 7
Santa Fe Pacific 113 (bottom), 132-33, 141 (top), 145 (both), 148-49
Southern Pacific 1, 45, 25 (both), 26-27, 27 (bottom), 30, 31, 32, 33 (both), 34, 35 (both), 36-37, 38, 42-43 (bottom), 44-45
46, 52, 52-53, 57, 60, 66, 66-67, 68-69, 72, 73 (all 3), 74-75, 75, 76,-77, 79, 80, 82-83, 84-85 (top), 84, 87, 88-89, 90, 91, 92-93, 96, 96-97, 104-05, 108-09 114, 114-15, 118-19, 120-21, 122-23, 124, 124-25, 125, 126-27, 128, 129, 138-39, 141 (top), 142 (top), 143, 147, 146-47, 152-53, 188-89, 188, 189, 192
Union Pacific Railroad 22, 24, 42-43 (top), 49, 65 (bottom), 70, 81
United States Envelope Co, Paper Cup Division 15
© Bill Yenne 28-29, 58-59, 62, 63, 98, 107, 110, 111 (both),134, (both), 181 (both), 184-85

Special thanks to Bob Sederholm at Southern Pacific, Pat Stafford at Burlington Northern, Bruce Harmon at FMC Corporation, Bill Burk at Santa Fe and our friends at the Alaska Railroad for their assistance in the photo research.

Page 1: An old 4-8-2 steam locomotive halts at the water tower.
Page 2-3: An Atchison, Topeka & Santa Fe freight pulls out of Flagstaff, Arizona on a snowy winter morning.
Below: A Canadian National freight heading west.

Contents

Getting up Steam

The successful use of steam power in the early nineteenth century ushered the Industrial Age into America. In particular, steam applied to railroads – hitherto pulled by horses – was a discovery which merged naturally with the promises and hopes of the fruitful land. The rambunctious nation would have a new horse to ride – the Iron Horse – which would go swifter, farther and cause more changes than any other means of transport. Indeed, the practical application of steam changed the nature of society as no comparable discovery had managed to since the invention of printing in 1444.

And yet, surprisingly enough, steam was not altogether a new story. Steam had been used to operate mechanical devices as early as in ancient Greece. Hollow statues of gods were attached to pipes hidden from public view. These pipes led down to underground fires which heated small amounts of water to steam. When the sufficiently credulous needed to be impressed, a priest could lift a lever, pushing steam through a trumpet-like aperture to create a godlike 'Yes' or 'No.'

Magical uses of steam were not carried over into Christian ritual, and the possibilities inherent in the force were consigned to a footnote of history until 1641 when the Marquis of Worcester made the rough Channel crossing from England to France to visit one Solomon de Caus. Solomon had written a book on the force of steam and its possibilities for practical application. Unlike Solomon's compatriots, who went so far as to declare the man mad and commit him to an asylum, the visitor listened attentively to his explanations. Upon his return to England, the Marquis enlarged upon the basic principles and ultimately built a

steam engine of his own. It was considered a toy, although the historian Thomas Macaulay noted skeptically that 'the Marquis had observed the expansive power of moisture rarified by heat. After many experiments, he had succeeded in constructing a rude steam engine, which he called a fire-waterwork, and which he pronounced to be an admirable and most forcible instrument of propulsion.'

In the new mood of scientific enquiry that overtook Europe in the seventeenth and eighteenth centuries, steam became a matter of increasing interest. Soon the idea that it was a possible source of energy was not to be scoffed at by even the most pragmatic. In 1759, the great inventor James Watt listened carefully to a Glasgow student. 'He threw out the idea,' Watt later wrote, 'of applying the power of the steam engine to the moving of wheel-carriages, and to other purposes.'

Watt worked out the principles of such an engine propelled by steam, but although he received patents for this in 1769, he was too busy to build it.

In France, meanwhile, the Marshall de Saxe had built just such a machine in 1763 with funds provided by the King. The engine had operated successfully, but unfortunately did not stop on command. It ran through a wall in its first demonstration. Instead of being provided with brakes, the machine was relegated to a museum.

None of these engines had the solidity of Oliver Evans' grandiosely named *Oruktor Amphibolus*. In 1772, four years before the War of Independence, the colonial American devised a 21-ton vehicle that looked more like a boat than a coach. A flat-bottomed, square vessel, it traveled on four wheels when on land, but was pushed by a paddle-

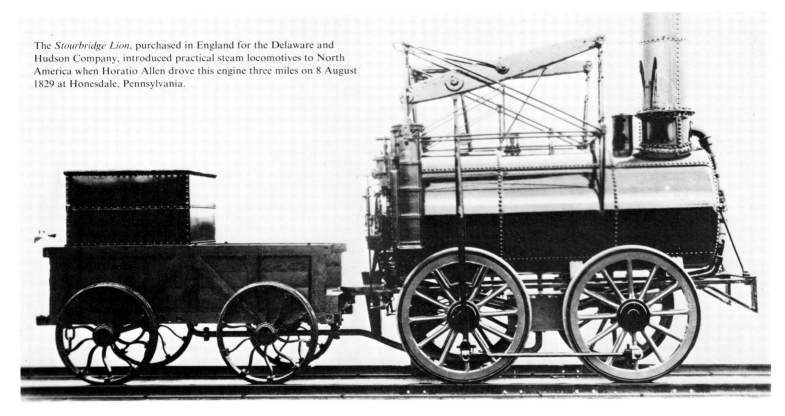

The *Stourbridge Lion*, purchased in England for the Delaware and Hudson Company, introduced practical steam locomotives to North America when Horatio Allen drove this engine three miles on 8 August 1829 at Honesdale, Pennsylvania.

wheel when on water. True to Evans' predictions, it puffed through the streets of Philadelphia, and paddled up and down the river, causing amazement and consternation. The Board of Health, which had commissioned the surprisingly successful engine, was now repelled by the ungainly creation and did not proceed with its use.

Evans was disappointed with the reception his invention received. He could clearly forsee the general use of steam. In 1813 he confidently predicted:

'The time will come when people will travel in stages moved by steam-engines from one city to another, almost as fast as birds can fly, 15 or 20 miles an hour.

To accomplish this, two sets of railways will be laid, made of wood or iron, on smooth paths of broken stone or gravel, with a rail to guide the carriages, so that they may pass each other in different directions and travel by night as well as by day; and the passengers will sleep in these stages as comfortably as they now do in steam stage boats.

Twenty miles per hour is about 32 feet per second, and the resistance of the air will then be about one pound to the square foot; but the body of the carriages will be shaped like a swift swimming fish, to pass easily through the air.

The United States will be the first nation to make this discovery, and to adopt the system, and her

The *Dewitt Clinton*, the first locomotive to be operated in New York State, was built at West Point Foundry. On 9 August 1831 this engine, with passenger cars resembling stagecoaches, made its initial run from Albany to Schenectady on the Mohawk & Hudson Railroad.

wealth and power will rise to an unparalleled height. I do verily believe that carriages propelled by steam will come into general use, and travel at the rate of 300 miles a day.'

If Oliver's prophecy did not seem altogether fantastical, it was because of momentous changes which had already occurred in his lifetime. In 1776, the United States had declared itself a new nation. In 1793, a deceptively simple mechanical device, the cotton gin, had been introduced into the manufacturing processes of the United States. After Eli Whitney's invention, American industry was never quite the same again. Cotton became a major crop and slaves a major business. The tragic issue of slavery assumed great importance in the subsequent development of the nation, especially of the South and West.

As a result of the Louisiana Purchase of 1803, the Mississippi had become a magical watery north-south road all the way to New Orleans – a trading port of utmost importance. The Mississippi, muddy and marvelous, was a veritable cornucopia of riches. However it also appeared an invisible wall separating the continent East from West. On the one side lay a burgeoning industrial civilization; on the other, an extremely dangerous unknown, called simply the Great American Desert.

It was steam that would make it possible to cross the barrier that the Mississippi represented; steam that would bring millions to populate the West; steam, which like some ancient genie, would transform the latent riches of the land into the lucrative markets that were soon to appear. The development of land on either side of the river would not fully take place until steel rails and intrepid railroad engineers supplanted the ancient Indian trails and legendary pathfinders.

When he put down his thoughts about the future of transportation, Oliver Evans was not a wild prophet. He now based his predictions on his own throughgoing work and also upon the steady development of the English railways.

In England, interest in a swifter mode of transportation came first from the collieries of their own West Country as new industrial processes increased the demand for coal. Initially, the solution was simply to lie in smoother roads such as John McAdam's hardtops, which increased the pulling power of the horse. Wooden tracks, and later iron ones, also made the hauling of even larger loads possible. However, it was soon clear that there was a need for some additional form of power besides the horse. In 1784, William Murdoch, who had been working with Watt, constructed a foot-high steam-carriage with three wheels. It was heated by a spirit-lamp. Murdoch tried it out one night after work, sending the sparking little machine down the darkened paths of Redruth in Cornwall. The high-pressure contraption tore away, Murdoch in pursuit. Hissing and sputtering away on its own, the errant machine

The *Tom Thumb* was constructed by Peter Cooper in 1829 and was the first locomotive to be built in the United States. On 28 August 1830 it became the first locomotive to pull a load of passengers when it hauled 18 directors of the Baltimore & Ohio Railroad from Baltimore to Endicott's Mills and back at speeds ranging from five to eighteen miles an hour.

PETER COOPER'S "TOM THUMB" 1829-30 BALTIMORE & OHIO R. R.

encountered the parish priest, whose howls of fear and dismay conveyed his conviction that the sudden appearance of this monster in the night must be the work of the devil. Murdoch was dissuaded from proceeding with his invention.

In 1801, the same year Thomas Jefferson was inaugurated President of the United States, Richard Trevithick (who had studied with Murdoch) constructed a simple four-wheel coach which ran on steam. It did not require tracks, but ran as an automobile might; it, too, was looked upon with dismay and apprehension. Trevithick drove the machine to London where it naturally caused quite a stir. On one occasion, the keeper of the tollgate addressed the inventor as 'Mr Devil,' allowing him to pass through without paying. Upon seeing the uncanny vehicle, the noted inventor, Sir Humphrey Davy, wrote: 'I shall hope soon to hear that the roads of England are the haunts of Captain Trevithick's dragons – a characteristic name.'

Trevithick, perhaps realizing that his contraption was being examined by some powerfully inventive minds, retreated to Cornwall to continue his work unobserved. There, he combined his discoveries as to the amount of weight which could be pulled over iron tracks with a new, more powerful steam engine. On 15 February 1804, he demonstrated his invention on a private coalyard track in South Wales. Trevithick had created the first fully operative steam engine ever to run on rails. It pulled five open coal

cars which carried some ten tons of bar-iron and 70 passengers over nine miles of track at the speed of five miles an hour.

There were serious drawbacks, however. Trevithick thought that smooth wheels would adhere to smooth track. He deemed it necessary to spike his wheels with protruding bolts and cross grooves. The ride was unnecessarily violent, wrecking the wooden tracks. In addition he failed to recognize the use of waste steam for quickening combustion by way of a steam blast out the chimney. The lack of these two all-important discoveries severely handicapped his engine. It was not much more efficient than a horse. It is not known why Trevithick did not pursue his experiments, for they were well on the way to solving the essential problems of steam locomotion on land. Still, it may in fairness be said that he produced the first true steam engine even though he failed to make it practical.

It was George Stephenson, an uneducated genius from the coal mines near Newcastle, who made the steam engine fully operational. Stephenson also saw the totality of engine, tracks, depots, supplies and passengers, which together would constitute a new industry called railroads. More importantly, he could claim credit for making this industry acceptable to financiers and public alike. It is for this fact, rather than for his outstanding inventive powers, that George Stephenson deserves to be called the father of the railroad.

Born in a small mining town of Wylam in northern England in 1781, George Stephenson went to work in the mines at an early age. His father earned 12 shillings a week; the family of eight lived in one room. Stephenson was illiterate until the age of 18. Then he hired a teacher to show him how to read. Already, his knack for machines had put him in charge of the colliery's stationary steam pumps and elevators.

In response to the rising demand for improved methods of transportation, Stephenson began to work on rail transport. Since interest in development lay primarily within the coal industry, Stephenson was in the right place at the right time. Building his own first major engine, the *Blucher*, in 1814, he had only the most primitive tools and, naturally, inexperienced workmen whom he drafted from their labors in the Killingworth coal mines. The head mechanic was borrowed from the colliery's blacksmith shop. Stephenson's engine was fairly crude. It had no springs; its draught became too hot; the engine's force was unevenly distributed so that it jerked uncomfortably. However, it was an auspicious beginning. He has used smooth wheels on smooth tracks, transferring to heavy locomotives a method already successful on horse-pulled tram lines. Stephenson now devoted himself to designing, refining and experimenting with other engines for work in the coalyards.

In 1825, Stephenson's gifted son, Robert, joined with his father to build the first full-fledged railroad: the Stockton & Darlington. This ran 12 miles from the colliery at Darlington to Stockton by the sea. Originally, the backers had been prepared to settle for horse power. 'A horse upon an iron road would draw ten tons for one ton on a common road,' it was said. But when George Stephenson made his case for his locomotives, 'there was such an honest, sensible look about him, and he seemed so modest and unpretending,' that he prevailed.

With sales for their locomotives now safely assured,

TEN MINUTES F

REFRESHMENTS.

Above: The *Atlantic* locomotive, shown here pulling two double-decked Imlay coaches, was built by Phineas Davis at York, Pennsylvania and went into operation on the Baltimore & Ohio Railroad in the summer of 1832. It is still in operating condition.

the Stephensons invested their own savings in a small factory to construct engines for the Stockton & Darlington project.

By 27 September 1825, the iron tracks and carefully engineered bridges, all designed by the Stephensons, were in place. The first public railroad opened to great fanfare. The eight-ton engine named *Locomotion* pulled a tender and 34 cars, weighing some 90 tons in all. It sometimes reached the speed of 12 miles an hour. The railroad's directors scrunched into one open carriage. Twenty-one more wagons were occupied by an unprecedented 600 passengers. The cars were fitted with temporary seats, but there were no coverings to protect passengers in the front carriages from smoke and cinders. Spectators lined the roadbed. A horse and rider led the engine, waving a red flag to warn people out of the way. Upon its arrival at Stockton by the sea three hours and seven minutes later, *Locomotion* was greeted with booming cannon, ringing church bells, crashing cymbals, drumbeats and trumpet blasts from local bands. Banquets and feasting followed the successful completion of the journey. Although still not truly competitive, Stephenson had demonstrated that the steam power would in the long run efficiently and cheaply replace horse power.

In spite of opposition from turnpike owners and canal operators, who had strong support from local innkeepers and merchants, steam engine development proceeded apace, refinements being added quickly and efficiently. Soon the need for some standardization became apparent. In the old English tradition of jousts by knights in armor, George Stephenson suggested an open trial for steam engines. Backers were found to put up a £500 prize, but

everyone knew that whoever won would gain more than money. World prestige was on the line. On 6 October 1829 enthusiastic young men from foreign countries, such as Horatio Allen from America, crowded the bannered field of Rainhill. They were all intent on learning of new developments in order to report back to their own companies.

Strict rules of competition had been set, among which were the following: the engine must be supported on springs, consume its own smoke, weigh no more than six tons, draw 20 tons weight at a minimum of 10 miles an hour. It must not cost over £550.

The Rainhill Trials, as they were called after the field where they took place, lasted a week and spread railroad fever throughout the world. Only three engines took part: Stephenson's *Rocket*, Timothy Hackett's *Sans Pareil*, and Braithwaite & Ericsson's *Novelty*. Pulling out all the stops, the Stephensons, father and son, drove their engine across the finish line at 29 miles an hour. By the end of the week-long trials, the *Rocket* was declared winner. Horatio Allen, for one, ordered three of Stephenson's engines for the Delaware & Hudson Canal Company.

The spectators at the Rainhill Trials on that day in 1829 also witnessed the first railroad accident when a Minister of Parliament, William Huskisson, was pushed by the crowd in front of the engine. His legs were badly crushed. George Stephenson himself fired up another engine and rattling away at 36 miles an hour, tried to get him to medical aid. In spite of the desperate heroics, Huskisson died. His life was the first of thousands to be sacrificed to the Iron Horse. Indeed, there was a time when the Iron Horse seemed to consume lives like so much fodder.

In America, the politics of transportation was set against the needs of a small population in a vastly rich, and often dangerous, continent. Capital poured into turnpikes and canals with an extravagance matched only by the exuberance of the project operators. Between 1812 and 1837, the

Above: This scene from a series of historical covers depicts a race between the *Tom Thumb* and one of the early horse-drawn cars used on the Baltimore & Ohio Railroad that took place on 25 August 1830 from Relay to Baltimore, Maryland.

halcyon days of canals, tranquility added to the pleasure of the passengers, but slowness added to the frustration of the merchant shippers.

But not for long. The shrill blast of the locomotive engine, an innovation provided by the inventive Mr. Stephenson, was soon to shatter the bucolic scenes along rivers and roads.

In 1825, the same year that Stephenson was building the Stockton & Darlington, the American inventor George Stevens constructed a small, circular cog-wheel track in his own garden in Hoboken, New Jersey, to demonstrate the feasibility of steam. Upon it he ran a tiny steam engine which he had built himself. Only five years later, his two sons were given a charter to build the first railroad in America: the Camden & Amboy between New York and Philadelphia. For this road, Robert Stevens devised the so-called T-rail, the all-important security development which holds rail wheels firmly on track. The brothers added a cow-catcher to the front of their engine to protect it from straying cattle, thereby creating the characteristic look of the American steam engine.

On 4 July 1828, even before the Camden & Amboy came into being, the Baltimore & Ohio had begun construction of a line to run from Baltimore, Maryland to Wheeling, in western Virginia. It was begun with a rowdy ceremony. Charles Carroll, the last surviving signer of the Declaration of Independence, was on hand to break the earth. It was to become an historic railroad, playing an important part in the Civil War. But it presented one formidable obstacle which had first to be overcome. At a place in the line called Rocky Point, near Harper's Ferry, Maryland, the track made a short turn of 150-foot radius. George Stephenson had stated flatly that no locomotive could draw a train of cars on any curve shorter than a 900-foot radius. Peter Cooper, who had invested heavily in the B&O, now stood to lose all unless he could solve the problem of the short turn. As he told the story,

'So I came back to New York and got a little bit of an engine, about one horse-power (it had a three and a half inch cylinder, and 14-inch stroke), and carried it back to Baltimore. I got some boiler iron and made a boiler, about as big as an ordinary washboiler, and then how to connect the boiler with the engine I didn't know.

I had not only learned coach-making and wood carving, but I had an iron-foundry and had some manual skill in working in it. But I couldn't find any iron pipes. The fact is that there were none for sale in this country. So I took two muskets and broke off the wood part, and used the barrels for tubing to the boiler, laying one on one side and the other on the other. I went to a coach-maker's shop and made this locomotive, which I called the "Tom Thumb," because it was so insignificant. I didn't intend it for actual service, but only to show the directors what could be done. I meant to show two things: first that short turns could be made; and, secondly, that I could get rotary motion without the use of a crank. I effected both of these things very nicely.'

The directors were convinced but the stagecoach interests thought perhaps they could discredit the new rival. Choosing a splendid grey horse to pull a car full of passengers, the would-be rivals challenged Peter Cooper and his little *Tom Thumb* to a race. With Peter himself at the throttle and his own carload of passengers to cheer him on, the grey horse and the Iron Horse started off. The grey took the lead as the little engine built up steam, but soon *Tom Thumb* chugged ahead. Then, disastrously, a leather band slipped off a drum affecting other important parts so that the engine lost power. The horse caught up, pulled abreast, and, galloping at full speed, left the forlorn Peter Cooper and his *Tom Thumb* far behind. The horse-drawn train won the dramatic race, capturing the imagination of artists and public. It even convinced the directors of the B&O that they should stick with horse-drawn trains, which they did for awhile. It did not stop the inevitable.

Almost a year later, in May 1829, Horatio Allen's engine, purchased from George Stephenson at the Rainhill Trials, arrived in New York. As was the custom, the engine was cheerfully colored, including a bright red lion's head on the front of the boiler, to go with its name, the *Stourbridge Lion*. Shipping it west to central Pennsylvania, Allen proceeded to demonstrate its marvels. To the consternation of would-be passengers, the wooden tracks upon which the train was to travel ran across a 100-foot-high hemlock trestle bridge spanning Lackawaxen Creek. The seven-ton engine appeared far too heavy for the wooden span which was considered safe for no more than three tons. Allen fired up the boiler, pulled the throttle-valve and headed off alone at 10 miles an hour. The bridge held, so he ran on happily for several miles, demonstrating to ecstatic farmers and townspeople alike the modern miracle of steam locomotion. Although the bridge had not collapsed, unfortunately the wooden rails had been somewhat chewed up

by the heavy engine. The *Stourbridge Lion* was never put to regular use.

Wooden rails covered with thin sheets of iron were known as snake rails. These were fairly dangerous because the iron had a habit of curling loose from the wood and snapping up through the floorboards. They would soon give way to rails made of Swedish malleable iron. After the Civil War, these in turn were supplanted by more permanent chilled steel in the still-familiar T-rail shape. The Charleston & Hamburg Line's *Best Friend* provided another first when its boiler blew up on 17 June 1831. This accident inspired public concern for railroad safety. Subsequently, the company inserted a protective car loaded with cotton bales between the engine and the passengers.

Passenger travel was still mainly done by stage coach, although canal barges offered bucolic journeys and created an entrancing way of life for many during their heyday. Canals had become one of the primary avenues of long-distance freight haulage, and remained so until 1840 when they began to be supplanted by railroads. Palatial steam boats also competed for freight and passengers going to the new frontier. To reach the Great Lakes, to reach the Ohio, to reach the Mississippi, became national obsessions. At first astounding engineering feats, such as the $5,700,000 Erie Canal which opened the Great Lakes to eastern markets, gulped most investment capital. But rail-

roads soon made canals obsolete. As the desire for rail-roads became a national mania, capital poured into development – an estimated $50 million for construction of the Erie Railway running roughly parallel to the Canal from the Hudson to Lake Erie. Millions came from state and local governments, as well as eastern capital.

Small towns were linked and turned into cities. By 1850 the combined population of such rail destinations as New York, Philadelphia, Baltimore and Boston had risen to 1,162,000 from some 343,000 in 1820.

Americans were also moving westward. By the time the Mississippi was bridged in 1853, there were roughly 10,000 miles of track on the eastern side of the river. The mid-West lacked not only capital but labor, and a settled population, too. Yet in the 1850s, steel tracks penetrated Illinois, Michigan and Wisconsin, as well as other states, gradually shifting the nation's center of gravity from the eastern seaboard toward the Mississippi Valley.

Travel by rail was not always comfortable nor very safe. However, it was as good as any according to the English visitor Joseph Biggs, who wrote, upon a visit in 1837,

> 'There is no country where you can travel with such facility and cheapness as in America. There are already railways throughout all the New England States to every town of importance, and some thousands of miles in progress in the South and West.

Below: DeWitt Clinton was put into service in 1831 and hauled a small train of cars designed after the fashion of the stagecoaches of the period.

Above right: Spouted kettles like this were used in the early days of railroading to supply drinking water for passengers.

Built in 1831, the *John Bull* operated on the historic Camden & Amboy
Railroad in New Jersey and later became a part of the Pennsylvania Railroad.
It is now permanently installed at the Smithsonian Institution in Washington.

The engineers seem to have the "power" under better control than we have; I have seen a train moving at the rate of 17 miles an hour stopped in 40 yards. The engine carries a sort of large shovel in front, which removes obstacles on the rails. Riding on the engine of a Washington train at night I saw a cow lying on the rails. We were upon her at once, and I expected a terrible concussion, instead of which the shovel scooped her up and carried her a few yards, when she fell off on the roadside and the train passed on scathless.'

The noted author Charles Dickens had a more detailed and colorful view of American railroad travel. He made his journey in 1842, and reports on a trip from Boston to Lowell, Massachusetts.

'There is a great deal of jolting, a great deal of noise, a great deal of wall, not much window, a locomotive engine, a shriek and a bell. The cars are like shabby omnibuses, but larger: holding thirty, forty, fifty, people. . . . The train calls at stations in the woods, where the wild impossibility of anybody having the smallest reason to get out, is only to be equalled by the apparently desperate hopelessness of there being anybody to get in. It rushes across the turnpike road where there is no gate, no policeman, no signal; nothing but a rough wooden arch, on which is painted "When the bell rings, look out for the Locomotive."

On it whirls headlong, dives through the woods again, emerges in the light, clatters over frail arches, rumbles upon the heavy ground, shoots beneath a wooden bridge which intercepts the light for a second like a wink, suddenly awakens all the slumbering echoes in the main street of a large town, and dashes on haphazard . . . down the middle of the road. There – with mechanics working at their trades, and people leaning from their doors and windows, and boys flying kites and playing marbles, and men smoking, and women talking, and children crawling, and unaccustomed horses plunging and rearing, close to the very rails – there – on, on, on – tears the mad dragon of an engine with its train of cars; scattering in all directions a shower of burning sparks from its wood fire; screeching, hissing, yelling, panting; until at last the thirsty monster stops beneath a covered way to drink, the people cluster round, and you have time to breathe again.'

If Americans were not overly concerned for their comfort when traveling by rail, they were not to be put off by considerations of safety, either. Across dangerous distances, the West continued to dangle its prizes before the dazzled eyes of the new nation. The Louisiana Purchase of 1803 had made the Great American Desert available for exploration. Annexation of Texas in 1845 brought it under the jurisdiction of the US Army, thereby making settling and exploitation of the area a great deal more secure. Moreover, the territorial war with Mexico (1846–1848) made apparent the urgent need for a fast communications system. Vast tracks of western land were bought by foresighted eastern companies to await development.

As early as 1832, some people had begun to agitate for pushing railroads all the way to the Pacific coast. One instigator was Asa Whitney who, in 1844, offered the government 16 cents an acre for nearly 78 million acres west of the Mississippi. He was turned down. Another was Thomas Hart Benton, who wanted the railroad to be built by the government so that the vast riches which were bound to follow on such a venture would not fall into the hands of only a few people. Public debate was on.

Then one significant day in 1848, not only canny speculators and quixotic dreamers but the whole weight of national interest shifted from the east side of the Mississippi to the west. Something had occurred which changed the face of the nation almost overnight: not surprisingly it was gold. In a placer creek near Sacramento, California, on Monday 24 January 1848, a grand-scale rancher named John Sutter was shown some glittering golden stones. Biting, hammering, even boiling in lye and bathing in acid, failed to crack or powder the nuggets. Gold it was. Try as he might, Sutter could not keep the secret. His workers abandoned his land to go and dig for gold of their own. Strangers trampled in with sieves and picks and little leather bags in which to stash gold nuggets. The word spread. Gold-seekers came from all over the world. By the end of the year 50 ships a month were leaving the East Coast for the long voyage around the Horn to California. When they reached San Francisco, many ships were abandoned by the gold-hungry sailors and left to rot in port. At one time some 500 lay crumbling in the harbor, many with their cargoes still intact. Later when land was at a premium, a number were run ashore to be leased for up to $3000 a month as shops and restaurants. During the first year, a quarter of a million dollars was picked up by some 10,000 'gold dusters.' The peak year of 1852 saw some $81 million worth of gold taken by 100,000 recently arrived adventurers.

More important for the future, gold lust brought settlers to the West. It was easy to see that a land so rich in minerals, furs and forests could not be left unpopulated or unprotected. It must have closer ties to the rest of the nation. What better way than chilled steel rails with their hot little puffing engines carrying freight from East to West and then back again to the rich markets of the East. Railroads would make even gold-mining seem a piker's game. The dream of spanning a continent with a railroad was beginning to take on substance. Western states, counties and townships gave money, loans and rights-of-way to almost anyone who would undertake to form a railroad company.

Finally drawn into the excitement, in 1850, President Millard Fillmore signed a bill introduced into Congress by Stephen Douglas, giving some 2,600,000 acres of public land to the Illinois Central Railroad to aid in its development. The land was offered in six alternate sections of 460 acres each for every mile built. Setting an important precedent, the federal government gave its lands, at 10 cents an acre, with only the requirement that the Illinois Central should construct 700 miles of railroad in six years with seven percent of the gross to be paid the State in perpetuity.

Many Americans have since looked back at this legislation and concluded simply that the Federal government got a bad deal. The land grant to the Illinois Central was the first of many federal land grants, a total of some 180 million acres by the time the aid stopped in 1872. These grants were a decisive factor in the financing and development of the western railroad systems.

From the perspective of over a century and a half, it would seem that Constitutional issues were at stake rather than mere investments. Once the plunge was taken these issues would not go away. Does the government have the right to finance private businesses? Are railroads, or any other national transportation systems, altogether private businesses? When the realm of public services becomes intrinsic to an industrial nation, where does the responsibility of government lie? The Illinois Central Federal land grant opened a Pandora's Box of Constitutional issues with which the country would still be struggling a hundred and fifty years later.

The day President Millard Fillmore signed the land-grant bill was a day of national rejoicing. Americans well understood that the Federal land-grant scheme would soon be stretched to include their state or territory. The prospect was intoxicating. There were spectacularly rowdy celebrations in California, which had so much to gain by a railroad link with the East.

On 9 December 1852, there was another occasion for festivities. The Pacific Railroad of Missouri steamed proudly out of St Louis to puff its full five miles toward the Pacific. The ride was another momentous milestone in the spread of rails. Once again crowds cheered and banners waved, bells peeled and cannon boomed, while grandiose speeches poured forth with the mellifluousness of alcohol, generous amounts of which were in evidence all day. The Iron Horse had smashed the invisible wall that divided a continent. The blue Pacific beckoned. There were only 1600 miles to go.

But on its way to the Pacific, the Iron Horse made a detour. It went by way of the Civil War. In the process it served to change the nature of a nation. Although the strategic factor of railroads was not immediately recognized, nonetheless, it is safe to say that railroads were one of the most decisive factors in the final outcome of the conflict. The Civil War in its turn served to impress the nation with the urgent need for a uniting transcontinental railroad. During and after the war, newly functioning American steel and other heavy industries developed out of the exigencies of war were ably prepared to help construct the binding iron road.

In 1821, 31 years before the Pacific Railroad of Missouri steamed out of St Louis, and four decades before the Civil War, Southerners had forced Congress to agree to the so-called 'Missouri Compromise.' Far from being a compromise, this measure injected slavery into the new territory of Missouri. In one bold stroke, Congress, although probably unwittingly, had established that it was the duty of the Federal Government not only to protect but to extend the 'peculiar institution' of slavery.

The country was caught in a Constitutional dilemma: could the federal government guarantee the rights of slavery and of freedom at one and the same time? The answer had to be a resounding 'No!' Even so, the inevitable conflict was delayed for 40 years.

During those four decades, 1821 to 1861, railroads transformed society. Rails were laid on lands east of the Mississippi with increasing rapidity. In 1830 there were only 23 miles of track. A year later the figure was 91 miles. In 1835, 1000 miles had been laid. Five years later 3000, and by 1860 the figure had jumped to 30,000 miles of wood or iron rails crisscrossing east of the Mississippi. Railroad maps were beginning to look like plates of spaghetti.

In ever-increasing numbers, meanwhile, Europeans arrived to populate the West. Very often they were inspired to come by the railroads themselves, which vigorously promoted the advantages of the frontier and vied with each other for the hardworking newcomers. In the 1820s, 129,000 immigrants arrived in the United States; in the 1830s some 540,000 joined the new nation. In the 1840s the figure tripled to over a million and a quarter. By the end of the 1850s, it had reached an astronomical 2,814,554. One after another, cities grew where rails met: New York, St Louis and far away Chicago became major rail centers, leaving once-thriving cities to crumble slowly into dusty small towns far from the railroads' whistle.

Northern industrialists proposed to supply their voracious industries with foreign labor. The immigrants could settle the land, work the factories, ride the railroads. It was good for business.

The South objected to the influx of foreigners. The slavers expected to do their business with the virgin plantations of new slave states and territories. In plain English, they proposed to supply slave labor from what were in effect human stud farms of the southeast. Now that the Missouri Compromise had put the Federal government *de facto* on the side of slavery, the great, still undeveloped territories of the southwest seemed a particularly appropriate market for the slave trade. Railroads would make transportation easy. Railroads routed from Missouri through Texas, New Mexico, Utah and into California would ensure the success of the slavers' plan. Without shame, slavers produced figures to show that it was cheaper to furnish southwestern plantations with new batches of slaves every seven years and work them to death, than to furnish decent working conditions. The procedure would ensure continued business. For this reason, the South wanted immigration slowed, if not stopped altogether. It looked upon immigration as unfair competition.

During these same four decades, as the frontier expanded west, the demand for better transportation systems became more vocal. Once the Pacific coast was reached, gold and silver were added to the siren calls of virgin forests, plentiful prairies, and rich rivers. The issue of a national railroad became of paramount importance. This sense of urgency was voiced by Colonel John J Abert, head of the Corps of Topographical Engineers: 'Unless some easy, cheap, and rapid means of communicating with these distant provinces

A woodburning steam engine of the 1854 era, uncoupled from its cars, pauses for fuel while a few friends stop to chat with the crew.

be accomplished, there is danger, great danger, that they will not constitute part of our Union.' Appreciating the risk, Congress took up the issue.

Stephen Douglas, the eloquent Senator from Illinois, proposed a northern route to run from the Great Lakes, via the mouth of the Columbia River, then through the Emigrant Trail at South Pass, then to Puget Sound. This proposal could boast the best port for ships going to the Orient, and excluded the solid South almost entirely from any benefits resulting from its construction. Since Congress was dominated by Southerners and southern sympathizers, Douglas had little chance of success.

An alternative route was proposed by Senator Thomas Hart Benton of Missouri. Not surprisingly he favored a starting point at St Louis, to follow the 38th parallel and what he dubbed the Buffalo Trail, proceed almost straight

over some of the wildest Rockies, across the hellish Great Basin, meet up with the Emigrant Trail over the Sierras, and continue to Sacramento and San Francisco.

There were two other possible routes, but only the Southern route had political backing. This route would go from Preston, Texas, through Mexican territory (unlikely as that might seem) to San Diego, California. It would bind California, Texas and everything in between solidly to the plantation South.

Responding to pressure, Congress authorized $150,000 for surveys to settle the vexed question. Appreciating the importance of the final decision, Secretary of War (and future president of the rebel Confederacy) Jefferson Davis, arranged to be put in charge of identifying the best route for a federally aided, continental railroad. Not surprisingly, a southern passage along the 32nd parallel seemed to him

the most practical. His highhanded 'Gadsden Purchase' even annexed a bit of Mexico (in return for a feather-smoothing $10,000,000) so that the tracks might pass directly west without passing through foreign territory.

Efforts to elicit the federal government's support for the fourth more natural central route (the one ultimately settled on), from Omaha through Salt Lake City, over the Rockies to the Humboldt River and from there to Sacramento, were continually thwarted by Southerners in Congress. Time and time again, the underlying cause of the controversy, slavery, prevented agreement. Not until 1862, when the Civil War was in full swing and the southern slave 'aristocracy' stood in defiance of the Union, did Lincoln sign a go-ahead measure authorizing the central route. Surveys were initiated at the time, but it was not until after the Civil War that construction began in earnest.

The Iron Road to the Golden West

No story of the railroad quite matches the drama of the planning and building of the transcontinental across the Rockies, the Sierras and the Great American Desert. Like some fantastical medieval legend, it is a saga which will be told and retold for years to come. The dreams, the plans, the heartbreaking and backbreaking work, the eventual broken promises, the improbable successes have become the stuff of legend – the great epic tale of the Iron Horse and the Early Industrial Age. The story has the stature of a morality play, but with a difference: is it an enterprising dream or a nightmarish enterprise? Who are the good guys and who are the bad guys?

The early Industrial Age produced some gigantic personalities. Few individuals in history have ever brought off such stupendous enterprises. One thinks of the irrigation canals of early Mesopotamia, the Pyramids of Egypt, the Panama Canal, and then, other than the massive movements of men at war, one finds little to compare to the mammoth undertaking of the builders of the transcon-

tinental railroad. More puzzling still, when one scrutinizes the original men who agreed to initiate the project while it was only a dream, one finds no distinguishing signs or portents to separate them from anyone else. They shouldered the burden of scouting the routes through the unknown, they inveigled the capital, corralled the labor, then kept the stupendous enterprise afloat while it snaked across the granitic heights of the snow-blanketed Sierras and Rockies. Yet scrutinized from another angle, the entire undertaking seems primarily motivated by greed. Only one active participant, the gentle, if persistent, Theodore Judah, saw the enterprise for what it was: the spine of a new nation. Upon meeting the other heroes of the Continental saga, one comes upon as mercenary a crew as are ever likely to stride from the pages of history.

Once the Civil War had been declared, politics were taken out of the eventual decision as to which route would be selected. The Emigrant Trail, already used extensively – it being the most sensible central route across Kansas – was picked without further argument.

The terrain to be traversed was exceedingly difficult and dangerous. There were indeed deserts out there, although it was not a great American Desert after all, being one of the richest areas in the world. Nonetheless, there was the Humboldt Desert to cross, alkaline flats that parched and killed almost all life, providing no wood for ties, no water for men. There were the Rocky Mountains, standing like giant knights in shining armor to prevent all passage. There were the Sierra Nevadas, mountains of an even harsher, harder sort, with walls of snow sometimes 100 feet deep guarded by sheer cliffs looming without footholds thousands of feet high. Everywhere the extremes of weather,

either baking the earth to a stone-like hardness, or freezing it to something resembling summit granite.

Of course, much of the land would be across the flat and fertile Kansas Territory which led all the way to the Rockies. Here, instead of inches, as at the top of Sierras, workers could lay seven and eight miles of tracks in a feverish day.

After years of stalemate, Congress had finally agreed to Lincoln's choice of the Emigrant Trail. Trains of covered wagons (built like boats to float across rivers) were already winding to the gold and silver mines of the far West. Sleek stagecoaches such as those of the reliable Wells Fargo & Company already carried gold and securities one way

Below: Construction forces of the St Paul, Minneapolis & Manitoba Railway (forerunner of the Great Northern) were photographed in 1887 in present-day North Dakota as they moved up to the railhead, accompanied by soldiers for protection against hostile Indians. The 'skyscraper' dormitory cars shown here had to be sawed down to tunnel size when they reached the mountains.

Above: This famous old locomotive of the Western & Atlantic Railroad (later the Nashville, Chattanooga & St Louis) on exhibition at Union Station in Chattanooga, is still in existence. It was captured during the Civil War on 12 April 1862 and then recaptured by the Confederates.

Below: The *General Sherman* was the first locomotive purchased by the Union Pacific Railroad. It was shipped by boat from St Louis in 1865.

across the continent, and mail (as gladly received as gold back west) the other way. The Emigrant Trail had also been the route of the legendary Pony Express during its brief but glamorous life from 1860 to 1862.

The Emigrant Trail crossed the Missouri River near Council Bluffs, Iowa. It followed the Platte River, of which one contemporary guidebook claimed that 50 miles of water on the upper Platte Ford was somehow poisonous. 'If you would avoid sickness, abandon its use,' the book advised. The trail continued along the Sweetwater River to cross the Rockies at South Pass. It then wound down to the fertile land around Great Salt Lake.

In 1846, the perspicacious, polygamous Mormons had already staked out this enticing area as their own. Interested in the growing income brought by mounting transcontinental traffic, their leader Brigham Young sought to have the railroad track go through his city. Disappointed when a more northern route was chosen, he nonetheless contracted for $2 million worth of labor to lay 100 miles.

The Emigrant Trail left Salt Lake, continuing to unroll westward onto the arid Humboldt basin, mile upon mile of corrosively dusty desert, where alkaline powder infiltrated into gear and lungs alike.

'Start at 4 – travel till the sun gets high,' advised Joseph Ware in his up-to-the-minute guidebook of 1849. 'Camp till the heat is over. Then start again and travel till dark.'

Upon reaching the Carson River at the foot of the Sierras, one diarist claimed to have traveled 700 miles without seeing a tree. 'Expect to find the worst desert you ever saw,' a kindly traveler warned, 'and then find it worse than you expected. Take water, be sure to take enough.' It was agreed by all that the worst part of the trip was the Forty-Mile Desert which stretched and burned between Humboldt Sink and the Sierra's Carson River. The desert was littered with the bleached bones of man and beast bested by the terrible terrain. However, in 1849 when gold fever overcame what might have seemed common sense, some 22,500 rough and rowdy gold-seekers had braved the dangers of this central route.

Among its other dangers, the trail traversed sacred Indian hunting grounds. The Indians had been pushed back across the Missouri and promised the land there in perpetuity. But many people already understood that in a land-hungry world, with immigrants now arriving from Europe by the thousands every year, such a promise was impractical. As the newspaperman Henry M Stanley wrote of the Indians: 'They move us by their pathos and mourn-

ful dignity, but half a continent could not be kept as a buffalo pasture and hunting ground.' Grenville Dodge was one who well understood this fact, and after his service as an Army general in the Civil War, he worked hard to make the trail safe for the white man, and for his railroad. Along with friends made in the service during the Civil War, including Philip Sheridan, George B McClellan, and George A Custer, Dodge went out of his way to bait the exacerbated natives, goad them into attack, then relentlessly hunt them down like beasts. Some of the least explicable battles of the Indian Wars were motivated by the desire to clear land for the railroads.

The Indians did what they could to protect their right to live in dignity. They fought, they bargained, they worked, they traded; they became friends – and they became enemies. The wagon trains were often under attack by Indians trying to stem the trickle that had become a flood through their land.

Whether the white man was brave or cowardly, honorable or dishonorable, ultimately nothing worked to the benefit of the Indians, for as the Indians later explained about the white men they dealt with: 'They made us many promises, but they kept only one. They promised to take our land, and they did.'

When Jefferson Davis had authorized surveys of the western trails, he had deemed the Emigrant Trail sufficiently well known not to warrant any further expenditure of the Federal government's $150,000 survey budget. He compiled instead 13 volumes of varied data on the lands to be traversed by three possible alternate routes: The Northern Route from Lake Michigan to Puget Sound; a second, serpentine Central Route from St Louis to Sacramento; a second southern route from Fort Smith, Arkansas, through the oven-hot pass at Needles, straight to Los Angeles. He left out his own preferred Southern Route from Texas to San Diego. Davis deemed this the obvious choice. His surveys were conducted purely in order to prove the inadequacies of alternative trails, not to demonstrate their strengths. Davis decreed that enough was known about the Emigrant Trail to warrant its exclusion.

The visionary young engineer Theodore Judah and the intrepid Grenville Dodge had both spent years surveying for possible railroad beds. They knew that the Emigrant Trail was the most logical route for the nation to construct upon. Judah had explored the wild Sierras, from Sacramento over the summit to the Truckee River near the California-Nevada border. Dodge had explored the Great

American Desert and had found the wild Lone Tree Pass through the Wasatch Mountains, not far from Salt Lake. Both had invested their lives in a dream. Both would help make their dream come true, although Judah would not live to see its completion.

When the young genius, Theodore Judah, read the 13 volumes of information which Jefferson Davis had gathered to help Congress make up its collective mind, he noted its general inadequacy. There was no data of any use to a railroad engineer: no data on cuts, profiles, gradings or fills; no precise information upon which to make accurate calculations and predictions of feasibility and costs.

Commenting on the Secretary's data, the young man explained himself in a pamphlet titled 'A Practical Plan for Building the Pacific Railroad':

'When a Boston capitalist is invited to invest in a railroad project, it is not considered sufficient to tell him that somebody has rode over the ground on horseback and pronounced it practicable. He does not care to be informed that there are 999 different varieties and species of plants and herbs, or that grass is abundant at this point, or buffalo scarce at that.

His inquiries are somewhat more to the point. He wishes to know the length of your road. He says, let me see your map and profile, that I may judge of its alignment and grades. How many cubic yards of the various kinds of excavation and embankment have you and upon what sections? Have you any tunnels, and what are their circumstances? How much masonry and where are your stones? How many bridges, river crossings, culverts, and what kind of foundations? How about timber and fuel? Where is the estimate of the cost of your road, and let me see its details?'

Theodore Judah knew what he was writing about. By the time he had reached the ripe age of 28, he had already engineered several eastern railways, including the breathtaking Niagara Gorge Railroad. Judah was born in Bridgeport, Connecticut in 1826. As fate would have it, his father, an Episcopal minister, died while his son was still in school. Theodore was forced to change his goals from a career in the navy to engineering. When the family moved to Troy, New York, the young man found work on a railroad being built from Troy to Schenectady. He fell in love with railroads with a passion that never wavered for the rest of his life.

In 1854, Judah was asked by the Sacramento Valley Railroad of California to make the long trek West and be their chief engineer. This meant transplanting himself and his wife, Anna, from Massachusetts to California at a time when capital for railroad building was flooding into the rail companies of the East.

The magic call of the golden West prevailed. The Sacramento Valley Railroad would be the first railroad venture in California, a prospect which delighted the romantic young engineer. He took the job. Judah already had a second dream, one which would overshadow the accomplishment of the splendid Niagara Gorge Railroad: it was the dream of a transcontinental railroad. Theodore Judah wanted to be the engineer of such a grand undertaking. He surveyed, fought, dreamed and convinced others of the need for a transcontinental railroad. More than any other man, he brought the shining dream down into the thick, often murky, atmosphere of reality.

Judah was not alone in thinking that without the aid of the Federal government, the project would not be brought off. From the vantage point of a century later, it would seem that the project might have been delayed no more than some 20 years, but in those 20 years what changes might have taken place? Many people felt that the far West might indeed be lost to the Union without a cross-country rail connection.

At the time there were only three tenuous links between the East and the far West. There was the land route already described, traversed by wagon trains and stage coaches. Strenuous enough for individuals, it was not practical for moving the large quantities required to build a true nation.

The cheapest way for goods and equipment to reach California was by way of the 13,000-mile sea journey around Cape Horn, a voyage usually spanning some 26 weeks, but often enough taking a full 12 boring and difficult months. If one were lucky, one might catch one of the new swift Clipper ships which decorated the great oceans so grandly for the brief time between 1850 and 1869.

The other preferred passage was across the isthmus in Nicaragua. It was more expensive (sometimes up to $1000 for a place in the hold) because of freight handling, and slightly more dangerous than the Cape because of the possibility of contracting yellow fever, but less time-consuming. It was far less onerous than crossing the Overland Trail by wagon.

Well aware of these rivals, Judah settled in to build the Sacramento Valley Railroad, which he immediately regarded as the first leg of a transcontinental railroad. The tracks ran through the main streets of Sacramento, on some 22 miles to Folsom. Folsom was the jumping off place for the nearby Sierra gold mines. But gold is mined, not farmed. Soon there was no gold left. People moved away and Folsom shrank. The railroad remained almost unused. Judah's dream that it was the 'grand avenue of approach to the metropolis of the Pacific' was abruptly derailed.

Undeterred, Judah sought backers for a larger dream: his transcontinental railroad. He found avid listeners. California wanted to be bound to the rest of the nation with iron rails. People came to hear his plans. Judah himself became obsessed with his idea. 'Crazy Ted Judah,' he began to be called. With the support of some enthusiasts, he returned to Washington in 1860 to try to hearten Congress into financing the enormous enterprise. The Civil War

interrupted his plans. Judah returned to his beloved Sierras to explore for a suitable pass. All the summer of 1861, he camped out, measuring, surveying, studying. It was not until he met up with Daniel 'Doc' Strong that the solution came to him. Strong was a pharmacist in Dutch Flats, a mining town in the Sierra foothills. He was also the local doctor (since there was no other choice), hence his nickname. Doc loved his town and had helped it prosper by discovering an easy wagon road running westward over the Sierras right to its door. He had also come across what he deemed the most likely route for a transcontinental railroad. It wound up a granite spur between the American and Yuba Rivers, rolled down relatively gentle slopes to the Truckee River, then stretched out into the arid flats of the Humboldt Basin.

Needing confirmation from a professional, Doc Strong took Judah over the trail, up to the top where it reached the old Emigrant Pass. They were so absorbed in their discoveries that the two explorers were caught out in a storm. They had to make the dangerous descent to camp in total darkness. But there was method in their madness. Both Doc and Crazy Ted knew they had found their railroad route.

They returned to Strong's pharmacy and carefully prepared the articles of association for the Central Pacific Railroad of California. The first leg of the magnificent struggle was over. The route over the seemingly impassable Sierras had been explored, and as far as engineer Judah was concerned, settled upon.

Now for money. To incorporate under the laws of California, Judah had to raise $150,000, $1000 for each of 115 miles to the California border. His never-failing optimism was now tested to the limit as he attempted to raise the needed capital. Dutch Flats merchants pledged $46,500 within three days. It looked easy. But then weeks of frustrating talks passed. Try as he would, the capital was tougher to chip loose than the granite at Summit Pass.

His wife, Anna, remembered him after one particularly disappointing time in San Francisco. 'On his return from the meeting his words of me were these: "Anna, remember what I say to you tonight, so you can tell me sometime: not two years will go over the heads of these gentlemen but they will give up all they hope to have from their present enterprises to have what they put away tonight!"'

It was not until he reached the very bottom of despair that his luck turned. Meeting after meeting had failed to

Left: Construction forces for the transcontinental railroad gather around the Paymaster's car to collect their wages, which averaged three dollars a day. One quarter of the force consisted of tracklayers; the rest included graders, herdsmen, cooks, blacksmiths and bridgebuilders.

Right: Collis Huntington was formerly a Sacramento merchant.

Below right: An annual pass on the Central Pacific, issued to J J Orr.

Bottom: During 1887, pioneer rail-laying gangs built 636 miles of track on the St Paul, Minneapolis & Manitoba Railway between Minot, North Dakota and Helena, Montana from 2 April to 19 November.

bring in the needed capital. Finally about a dozen men gathered over a hardware store owned by two merchants, Mark Hopkins and Collis P Huntington. They were joined by Doc Strong and friends of the store owners, James Bailey, a jeweler; Lucius Booth, and two railroad promoters, the brothers Robinson. A surveyor named Leete and Cornelius Cole, who later became a US Senator, augmented the gathering. More importantly, two others joined the unlikely group: the drygoods merchant Charles Crocker and the grocer-politician Leland Stanford.

Having learned a hard lesson, Judah deliberately refrained from emphasizing the transcontinental aspect of his dream. Instead he spoke to the nearsighted goals of his small-town listeners. He proposed a road that would carry equipment over to the new silver mines of Nevada; it would augment property values, monopolize trade, save millions of dollars for the denizens of the mining towns. Judah did not try to inspire great visions of transcontinental railroads designed to benefit, even create, a nation. He knew his audience. He appealed to their profit-oriented instincts as merchants. 'Why, you can have a wagon road if not a railroad,' he explained, outlining the benefits of a proper survey over his projected route.

This time Judah did not fail. The merchants subscribed the minimum needed and the Central Pacific Railroad was launched.

Only one member of the audience held out: the shrewd Collis P Huntington. Judah went to speak to him the next day, looking for additional cash to begin a detailed engineering survey. Huntington could see a good deal, waiting, like a ripe fig, to be picked. He would go into the company, he explained, finding another six friends to help pay for a working survey across the mountains. In return Huntington asked for some rich rewards. He and his friends would be controlling officers of the company.

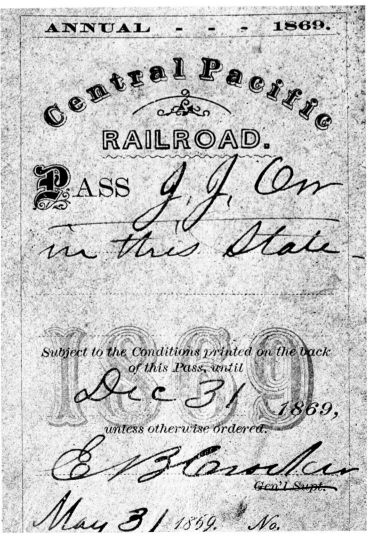

ANNUAL - - - 1869.

Central Pacific RAILROAD.

Pass *J. J. Orr*

in this State

Subject to the Conditions printed on the back of this Pass, until

Dec 31 1869,

unless otherwise ordered.

E B Crocker

Gen'l Supt.

May 31 1869. No.

26

Above: Leland Stanford, first president of Southern Pacific.

Right: Chinese workmen, using pick and shovel, one-horse dump carts and black powder, carve their way through and over the granite Sierra Nevada mountains in California, preparing the way for the 690 miles of rails of the Central Pacific from Sacramento to Promontory.

He designated Leland Stanford president; Huntington himself to be vice-president; his friend Bailey secretary; his partner, Mark Hopkins, treasurer. The others were to be placed on the board of directors. It was agreed that Judah's share of stock would be in recompense for his part as surveyor and initiator of the project.

Judah did not mind losing a place as an officer. His dream was to be Chief Engineer of the transcontinental railroad. He did not forsee what abdicating power would mean to his future. Indeed, one wonders whether Judah got his nickname 'Crazy' Ted more for his lack of interest in power and money than for his single-minded concentration on his goal.

This easily the legendary Big Four, Huntington, Hopkins, Crocker, and Stanford became officers of the new company. The others soon slid off the tracks of history, but these four became household words, names spoken at first with awe, but ultimately with the utmost hatred.

Whatever the limits of its initiators, one of the most astounding enterprises of the ages was begun that night over the Sacramento hardware store. However unsavory, the Big Four subsequently embodied the shimmering American Dream that anyone, be they ever so humble, unworthy, or uncouth, can make good – that is, become rich.

Judah was happy. His own dream was also coming true. He had raised the necessary money for incorporation. He had gathered sufficient funds for a working survey. He had prepared an exceedingly accomplished survey of his proposed route. In it he showed how to overcome obstacles presented by a summit of some 7000 feet to be reached in less than 20 miles; how to deal with heavy winter snowdrifts which would require sometimes 15 engines to push a plow through; how to fill or trestle deep canyons; penetrate miles of dense granite for tunnels; how to carry out the work in adverse weather conditions.

Above: Mark Hopkins co-owned a hardware store with Collis Huntington.

Below: A Chinese tea carrier delivers tea to the workers on the line 105 miles from Sacramento. Chinese work gangs set up their own kitchens and were fed dried fruit, vegetables and tea. Consequently, they seldom suffered from dysentery or scurvy as did the Caucasians.

Judah, just turning 36, was indefatigable in pursuit of his goal. The next step was to involve the Federal government. For this purpose, Judah returned to Washington, accompanied by Collis Huntington. Both set about lobbying Congress for help.

Judah set up a small railroad museum in his office, expostulating on the glories of a transcontinental to anyone who would listen. He also managed to get himself made secretary of the Senate Railroad Committee and clerk of the House Committee on Railroads. He had the privilege of the floor of the House, and a voice in all proceedings. Although not an elected official himself, he took part in writing the Pacific Railroad Act of 1862, which a willing wartime Congress eagerly passed and which Lincoln signed as enthusiastically on July 1. It authorized the Central Pacific to build from the West. It chartered a new company, the Union Pacific, to build from Omaha. Later, when a dangerous rivalry arose as to where the tracks would

Below: A temporary and permanent bridge under construction with Citadel Rock in the distance.

meet, it was arranged that they meet at Promontory in Utah, 40 miles northwest of Ogden. The right-of-way to a strip of land was granted, plus for each mile 10 alternate sections of land lying along the tracks. In addition, a loan would be forthcoming of $16,000 for every mile laid on flat land, $32,000 for tracks laid in the foothills, and a whopping $48,000 for the arduous work across the high Sierras and Rockies. The money would not be paid over until the first 40 miles of track were operating.

Judah was ecstatic. 'We have drawn the elephant,' he wired his partners, happily. 'Now let us see if we can harness him up.'

Judah resigned his Congressional committees and became Chief Engineer for the Central Pacific railroad. His dream seemed to have come true. The visionary went to work with the four merchants, he to build the best railroad possible, they to build a fast (and, if necessary, shoddy) road to pry loose the first of the fabulous windfalls promised by the Railroad Act.

A showdown between the two parties was inevitable. It began when the directors decided to lay new track to Folsom, crisscrossing instead of buying the Sacramento Valley Railroad already built by Judah; each new mile meant government land, loans and money. The irreparable break, however, came over where the Sierra baseline began. The Big Four brought in geologists to swear that the Sierras began some 25 miles before any perceptible rise in the landscape.

In Washington, Huntington had his seemingly bottomless slush-fund to help Congressmen see the Central Pacific's point of view. Lincoln, preoccupied with war and in a hurry for the transcontinental to get on its way, approved the choice. It meant an awesome million dollar difference. Representative Aaron Sargent of California explained how it worked: 'Here, you see, my pertinacity and Abraham's faith moved mountains.' Judah was incensed. He had an argument with the Four and seems to have gotten an agreement to buy out the partners. He then took passage across the isthmus to New York. His plan was to raise capital and build an exemplary road. Eastern financiers were already interested. But Judah's role in the unfolding drama was over. He contracted yellow fever in Nicaragua, and died en route to New York.

'Crazy Ted Judah' had surveyed the dream. It was left to others to drive the last spikes in place.

Who were the men who would tap in the last gold and silver spikes and reap the rewards? In colloquial American style, they were dubbed the Big Four. As if by chance, they acquired more wealth and power than dreams are made of. They complemented each other, forming a strong partnership about which they were characteristically reticent. They indulged in no public squabbles, betrayed no confidences, kept few records with which to 'follow me through life by the quarters I have dropped.' Each having the single-minded drive of a Napoleon, these four ruthless men paradoxically bent their considerable energies to one of the

most constructive enterprises of all time. Later all four created what was seen as a competition-strangling 'Octopus,' the rail network in California. Whatever the undertaking, they remained loyal, if not truly friendly to each other, to the end of their days.

The least prepossessing of the Big Four was austere, methodical Mark Hopkins, an accountant by temperament and trade. Older than his partners, he was born in Henderson, New York in 1813. Going West to California, he joined up with Huntington in 1856 to keep accounts for their hardware store. Sometimes called 'the stubbornest man alive,' he was one of those men of simple tastes, who make it big and never change their habits. Even when he was worth some $20 million, he continued to keep accounts of his vast empire himself, as if still taking a weekly check on the old hardware store. He remained in his same apartment in the less affluent side of town, growing his own vegetables. He kept his wife living frugally. Finally she prevailed upon him to move to something more commensurate with their wealth. With his grudging approval she then spent millions for a house built to her specifications on Nob Hill in San Francisco. He called it 'Hotel de Hopkins' and continued to grow his own turnips in the garden. With his microscopic gaze fixed on every penny, he was not only a trial for his wife, but for all of California as well.

His partner Collis P Huntington was the architect of the Big Four's colossal railroad empire. He was a tireless worker, often vindictive, essentially a loner. He was once

Opposite left: Builders remove dirt from the 90-foot-high Secrettown trestle in the Sierra Nevada mountains of California in 1877 that was filled in by the Central Pacific Railroad. Builders had only meager tools with which to blast through the mountains for the first transcontinental railroad.

Above: Central Pacific's first locomotive, the *Governor Stanford,* in the railroad's Sacramento yard along Front Street during construction around 1864, was photographed by Alfred A Hart, the official Central Pacific photographer. Locomotive No 1 was too light for heavy operations on the steep grades of the Sierra Nevada Mountains. She was soon delegated to local work as a Sacramento switch engine and is one of the two engines from the first transcontinental railroad that still exists. To the left is one of the first coaches in service, far more ornate on the interior, but similar to the Southern Pacific 71 still in existence in Sacramento. In front of it is a two-man hand-pump car. On the right, fronting on the Sacramento City Water Works – which was to be rebuilt as the Sacramento City-County Museum – are lengths of 56-pound iron rail waiting to be shipped to the railhead, at that point near Newcastle in the Sierra foothills. Rails, spikes, locomotives, freight cars and hundreds of other items used in railroad construction had to be built in factories in the East, disassembled when necessary, brought to seaboard ports by rail or wagon and loaded onto ships that transported them 15,000 miles around Cape Horn at the foot of South America to the West Coast. In San Francisco they were loaded onto riverboats and taken to Sacramento for reassembly or delivery to the construction front. The fireman standing in the center of the group with a mallet in his hand has just filled the engine with wood and he is conferring with the engineer, who consults his watch. Excess wood is on the hand cart in the foreground. The bridge in the background is the first bridge across the Sacramento River. It was built in 1857 and was replaced by the California Pacific Railroad Bridge in 1870, one year after the completion of the Central Pacific.

32

described as 'ruthless as a crocodile.' Methodically, he learned the necessary lessons well. He once spent $11,000 to be taught how to lobby Congress. From then on he seldom had less than $500,000 to spread around Washington at his discretion.

Huntington was born in Harwinton, Connecticut in 1821. He was the son of a tinker. A variety of jobs taught him a variety of ways to accumulate profits. He went west, lured by gold in 1849. He later looked upon the half day spent digging for gold as the one day he wasted in his life. He then put his capital into a hardware store, perceiving that whether gold or silver was found, the means to dig for it was always needed. 'I kept my warehouse full when prices were low, and when they went up I sold out.' It was a simple formula. He was 'a hard and cheeky old man, with no more soul than a shark,' said a contemporary.

It was Huntington, considered to be the 'brains' of the Big Four, who masterminded the corporate arrangements which made them all rich. Once the enterprise was on its way, he stayed east much of the time, keeping a sharp eye out for rivals. He helped steer the Railroad Act of 1862 through Congress and helped get its even more generous revisions passed in 1864. He then remained east, taking responsibility for acquiring locomotives, rails, nails and equipment of all kinds, to be shipped round the Horn to his rail terminal in Sacramento. In this Huntington was something of a genius. It was no easy task in wartime. He could corner nails or locomotives at low prices when there was a constant strain put upon suppliers by the needs of the military. He also had to contend with wartime inflation. A small locomotive cost $13,000 where a big one had brought only $10,000 a year earlier. When an embargo on English rails passed Congress, rails rose from $55 per ton to $262. It has been estimated that the embargo added $20 million to the cost of construction. Even to book space on the steamships and clippers took all his talent. That construc-

tion never stopped for want of the necessary equipment was due to Huntington's constant vigilance.

When the transcontinental railroad was finished, Huntington continued to live in Washington. He continued to provide the political expertise needed to protect and expand the Big Four's monopolistic railroad empire. Amassing was an instinct of his, just as it was of his partner, Hopkins. Whereas Hopkins amassed money, Huntington collected railroads. Money followed.

The third partner of the amazing foursome was Leland Stanford, of whom it was said 'no she-lion defending her whelps or a bear her cubs will make a more savage fight than will Mr Stanford in defense of his material interests.'

Like the others, Stanford came from the East. His father was a farmer-innkeeper in Watervliet, New York when Leland was born in 1824. He had moved out to Sacramento in 1852 when he was 28 years old, where he joined his brothers in their grocery store. Sticking to his shop, he rode the crest of the 1849 gold rush, amassing a comfortable income. He also loved politics. He helped form the Republican Party in California. In 1861, he was elected Governor of California in time to throw the weight of the State behind his Central Pacific project. He got his State legislature to fork over $3 million by literally tossing gold pieces to the voters congregating near polling booths. In his own persuasive way he encouraged counties to ante up thousands more. San Francisco was induced to make a subscription of $1 million, which it later much regretted.

Stanford loved a good ceremony and could give a properly patriotic speech. The partners decided he was their representative to the people. Stanford spoke slowly, giving his listeners a sense of his thinking things out. Crocker sometimes thought him merely 'dimwitted.' Huntington claimed he had contributed once only to the Central Pacific. That was when he turned the first shovelful of earth to begin construction. He also presided over the joyous laying of the last tie at Promontory, Utah, where he was scheduled to hit the last, the golden spike from California. (He missed, much to the great amusement of the onlookers.) However, it did not hurt to have the Governor of your state on your board of directors. Most especially when he understood you so well. Neither Huntington nor Crocker ever publicly objected to so powerful an ally.

The last member of the legendary four was Charles Crocker. He was without doubt the most colorful of them all. Stanford the politician, Hopkins the accountant, and Huntington the mastermind-salesman all played important parts in the great undertaking, but Charles Crocker was the man of action who got the tunnels blasted, the tracks laid, the railroad built. Crocker, weighing in at some 265 pounds, was the bullwhip. 'Everyone was afraid of me,' he boasted, happy as a child in a sandbox.

Born in Troy, New York, on 16 September 1822, Crocker was already helping to support his mother and sister when he was 12, his father and brothers having gone west to establish themselves on the expanding frontier. When gold was found in California, Crocker followed the Overland Trail west. It was during this trek that Crocker discovered something about how others saw him. 'They would all gather around me and want to know what to do,' he ex-

Above: Governor and Mrs Leland Stanford, Sr at the laying of the cornerstone of Leland Stanford, Jr University in Palo Alto on 14 May 1887. At this time Stanford was a US senator but he had served as governor of California (1861–63) and was stilled called 'Governor.'

Left: Charles Crocker's mansion was destroyed by fire in 1906.

plained. He enjoyed the role of leader so naturally thrust upon him.

Crocker was not successful as a gold-seeker. Instead he teamed up with a brother who had already begun a dry-goods store in California. Soon they had three stores, including one in Sacramento. His career measuring out materials for the ladies of the coast was often used to caricature him in later times. He also became an alderman in the New Republican Party, where he met the three men so important to his subsequent career: Mark Hopkins, Collis Huntington and Leland Stanford.

On 8 January 1863, when Governor Stanford had dug his epoch-making shovelful to begin the western end of the transcontinental railroad, Crocker had already resigned from the board of directors of the Central Pacific. He was now president of his own Contract & Finance company. Not by chance he had Hopkins, Huntington and Stanford as silent partners. The company was set up to contract for constructing the transcontinental rail. It could charge whatever the traffic would bear, since the directors of the

one company would be paying themselves as directors of the other. The idea was not original with the four, but it resulted in a $63 million clear profit in addition to the cool million which the CP stock was valued at.

Honest Ted Judah insisted on giving contracts to other businessmen, and for a short stretch this was tried. It soon became apparent that these entrepreneurs did not have enough capital to work with, usually running out of funds before completing their one or two miles. The Contract & Finance Company had no such problem, dipping freely into CP pockets. Later when Congress sought to investigate the relation of the two companies, it turned out that an 'accidental' fire had providentially destroyed all the records. It is unlikely they would have been very enlightening. Each partner claimed to have turned over to the new venture his own money as needed. Each kept his own accounts. Profits were divided evenly. Huntington said that he signed for some $7 million which he did not own in order to promote needed capital. At one point the partners agreed to pay interest on all stock issued. Charles Crocker later claimed to have tried to sell out many times, but found no takers. 'That was the time when I would have been very glad to take a clean shirt and lose all I had, and quit.'

When one begins to add up the money pouring in from big towns and little ones, from state and federal treasuries, from freight haulage and land-grant sales, one finds it difficult to substantiate the claim that the officers of the Central Pacific were ever much at risk. Be that as it may, once the project was underway, Big Charley Crocker found his place in life. From then until the tracks met at Promon-

tory Point six years later, Crocker could be found somewhere near the railhead. He claimed he could wake up in his train at night and tell where he was on the line just by feeling the bumps on the road.

Boastful, bullying, crude, loud, vulgar, he kept 10,000 men and 600 teams working like one machine for almost six years. He had boundless energy. Nothing interfered with his single-minded goal of laying tracks. Neither 45-degree weather, nor 100-foot snowdrifts, avalanches, nor even the fact that sometimes at the rarified 6000-feet level, there was not even a ledge to stand on where the track must be laid and locomotives must puff.

While the other three partners dealt with the problems of gathering capital, Crocker concentrated on forging his crew into a powerful unit. He tolerated no complaints, no slacking. Often the work went on around the clock in three shifts. If anyone wished to leave, they were free to do so. There just was no transportation. With a timely sense of the dramatic, Crocker undertook to dispense the monthly pay himself, usually riding to the railhead on a donkey. With a sack of gold on one side, and a sack of silver on the other he carefully measured out the wages: $30 a month, or $1 a day, plus board for all workers.

Horses pulled small dumpcarts, while thousands of men pushed tiny wheelbarrows. These plus picks and shovels were the only tools used to fill ravines, clear out the deep cuts through the mountains and scrape the tunnels clean.

Early on, the Central Pacific bosses found that the Chinese were excellent workers. They were brought in because labor was as short in California as in any part of the frontier. Gold, independent businesses, mortgage-free farming, and mining attracted the adventurous, the strong,

the independent. Crocker siphoned off as many Chinese as he could from the cities of the West. Then, when they worked out so well, he brought them by the thousands from Canton province in China. They were known as 'Crocker's pets.' By the time the tracks were snailing across the Sierra summit, some 7000 Orientals were picking and shoveling for the railroad. Since no women were brought over, the men learned to take care of themselves, cooking, cleaning and being generally self-sufficient. Also among them were many excellent doctors. This made them admirable members of the rail camps. Later they would use their skills in the restaurant and laundry establishments which would become a familiar aspect of American cities and towns.

Getting right to work, Crocker set a ferocious pace from the start. By mid-summer 1863, the line was hauling freight and, for ten cents each, passengers the 31 miles to New-castle. In 1864 the more-than-lucky four received another bonanza. In order to induce eastern capital into the Union Pacific Railroad Company, which had been chartered to begin building from Omaha westward, Congress renegotiated its already glittering offerings. Union Pacific Vice-President Thomas Durant was in Washington with a half a million dollar 'suspense' fund; Huntington's quarter of a million more was also having its effect. A liberal Congress doubled its already generous land-grant giveaway to the Central Pacific and the Union Pacific impartially. The number of shares in the Union Pacific was increased to 1 million not to be sold below $100 par, but without limits as to how much any one person could subscribe. The deal was designed to benefit the stalled Union Pacific. It must have brought chuckles of glee to the California four. Once again the profits would be all theirs.

By January 1866, with 7000 Chinese and 2500 whites at work, the railhead was well along the steep climb to the frigid 7000 foot summit of the Sierras. The men lived in tents and shanties both winter and summer. Bonfires kept them warm. Sometimes, to the consternation of the bosses, wooden railroad ties valued at $8 each might be burned cheerfully in the snowy night. Danger from avalanches was ever present. Four times entire camps were swept away by avalanches.

Cape Horn was one of the more incredible construction feats the crew achieved. It was a sheer cliff from which a ledge – just large enough for an engine and its train to fit – needed to be chipped out. Since there was nowhere to stand, workers were lowered hundreds of feet on ropes. They swung some 2500 feet over the abyss. Because of their skill with explosives, the Chinese were conscripted for the next difficult task: to make small holes in which to push black powder, light it, then signal quickly to be pulled out of the way of the ensuing explosion. They became so fearless in this that they were soon digging several holes, filling them at the same time, then with extended fuses, arranging to have explosions at intervals, like fireworks. Incredibly, not a life was lost across the formidable cliff.

By 4 July 1866 the iron road had reached Dutch Flats, still on the western side of the summit. The Big Four had originally infuriated Judah by proposing to build only to Dutch Flats and simply take advantage of the freight monopoly that would then be theirs. Despite the fact that the country expected them to build a transcontinental railroad, the fact that trans-Sierran stage coaches carrying passengers to and from the mining towns would meet up with their track made many Californians suspiciously sure

Opposite top: A Central Pacific excursion train steams through rough terrain 57 miles from Sacramento.

Above: Central Pacific workforces lay track in Nevada during 1868 for the western link of the transcontinental railroad. Gangs of Chinese laborers followed the rail layers in the foreground to space and spike the rail to the ties. The rail was half as long and less than half as heavy as that in general use today. An all-time track-laying record, surpassing the previous Union Pacific record of six miles, was set by the Central Pacific men on 28 April 1869. In a carefully organized effort, ties were spaced along the graded roadbed for some distance ahead and rail hauled to strategic spots. Work started at sunrise and by sunset the gang of eight Irish rail layers and a small army of trackmen had completed 10 miles and 56 feet of track.

Below: Central Pacific's locomotive No 63, *Leviathan*, advances over a flat stretch near Deeth, Nevada. Mt Halleck is in the distance.

the rails would end there. It would mean a lucrative monopoly for the railroad. 'The Great Dutch Flat Swindle,' California newspaper headlines shouted, briefly cheering the overland stage coachers, steamers, and others soon destined to be ruined by the rails.

Perhaps, at first, the Big Four had not intended to proceed any further than Dutch Flats. Profits had been the yardstick for their small businesses, and profits would continue to be their yardstick, no matter how big they grew. However, once at Dutch Flats, with their well-oiled organization in place, they could see that profits lay ahead on the projected line like gold nuggets for the taking. If they only reached the California-Nevada line at the Truckee River, they would then be able to monopolize the road to the Nevada silver strikes such as Mother Lode and Comstock. That was something the merchants could understand. Once again they would control the trade; they alone would rake in the profits, charging what the traffic would bear.

So they pushed up into the barren, frozen heights of the Sierras. By November 1866, the track had reached some 6000 feet almost straight up. Trestling, bridging, and tunneling had made the grades negotiable. Nearly 3400 feet had been climbed in 28 miles. The 15 miles from Colfax to Cisco cost $8,290,790. Here the Overland Stage from the East connected with the train for the first time. Now freight from the Nevada silver mines began to be carried by rail.

The next leg of the journey was the hardest. There were more cuts to make, bridges to build and 10 tunnels to bore. Summit Tunnel alone was a quarter of a mile long. Its solid, frozen granite would have to be chipped out by hand. Progress was an average eight inches per working night and day. It took a full year to complete. The tunnel was worked from four sides, sleds carrying men and equipment to camps on the eastern end. A third camp was set up in the middle where a hole was opened so that Chinese workers could dig from the center in both directions. The volatile new mixture, nitroglycerine, was tried, but caused horrible accidents. Black powder was consumed at the rate of $54,000 a month.

At Summit Pass, Crocker made one serious error of judgment. When offered the chance to try a new-fangled gadget called a power drill, he turned down the offer. In spite of pleas from his partners, he refused to experiment, losing valuable time and money for his hardheadedness.

Up in these wild reaches of the Sierras, more than half the men were kept busy just shoveling snow. Sometimes to clear the tracks it might take four or five, once even 15, locomotives to push a specially designed plow through the 40, 50 and 60-foot drifts. To add to their woes, the 1866–1867 winter was one of the worst on record. To protect themselves and keep working, the men tunneled deep under the snow. For months, 3000 laborers lived and worked in the eerie light of their snow towns.

When the weather cleared, it took 300 men 10 days to clear one mile of magnificent primeval forest, the trees being seven and eight feet in diameter. Of the 40 miles at summit level, 37 miles needed to be covered by specially engineered, timber snowsheds, constructed to keep snow off the tracks so that travel could be continued throughout the winter months. It cost an additional $2 million. Lumber towns had to be established for the purpose, equipment brought the long journey round the Horn to the icy heights. Still using picks, shovels and wheelbarrows, the Chinese

The railroad yard at Truckee, California, shown here in 1864, was a busy spot during the construction of the first transcontinental railroad. Locomotives burned wood in those days, and a screen at the top of the large bonnet-type smokestacks kept sparks and wood cinders from flying out and setting fire to the countryside. Regular train service was inaugurated to Truckee on 3 April 1868, although there had been much activity there in prior months when advance construction work was pushed in Truckee Canyon while the Sierra region was covered with snow.

often took weeks just to clear cuts of ice sometimes 15 feet thick over the tracks.

Work on the eastern slope was begun at the same time. Equipment, supplies and food had to be brought over the summit on sleds during the harsh winter months and throughout the dangerous months of melting spring snows. Three locomotives, iron for 40 miles of road, and 40 freight cars were transported by sled to the men already working on the eastern downgrade which would require nine additional tunnels. By the end of the year the tracks had inched some 16 miles eastward over from Cisco, two miles over the summit.

It took two years to scale the inhospitable Sierras above Donner Lake. By the end of 1867 some 40 miles of mountainous road had been finished. Inch by inch, 12,000 half-frozen railroad men had carved deep cuts like the 800-foot-long, 63-foot-deep cut through Bloomer Pass; the ledge at Cape Horn where men began without even a toehold,

hanging 2500 feet over the American River; plus 15 tunnels including the quarter mile bore at Summit Pass. It was, without doubt, an incredible feat.

Costs which had been high at first, became astronomical. Hay for the horses had risen to $100 a ton. Everything else was commensurate. Chief Engineer James Strobridge guessed later that if the maniacal speed had not been an issue, cost could have been scaled down some 70 percent. As it was it cost an estimated $23,650,000 to reach the Nevada border.

By the time the men reached the Nevada border in June 1868, they were seasoned workers. Their bosses knew how to build railroads. Nothing could stop them now. Eagerly they looked toward the final leg of the race across the Humboldt Flats to Salt Lake. Profits and monopolies were still the name of the game, but now finally the Big Four could see the bigger game that Judah and Dodge, Whitney, Durant, Benton, Douglas, Lincoln and even Jefferson

Davis in his own historical way, had seen so clearly many years before. For them, the grandeur of the project, the benefits to their society, the bounties to their nation were part and parcel of the enterprise. The Big Four had doggedly concentrated on profits. Now, finally profits included the transcontinental dream.

Each scorching mile now meant a profit of twice its cost, so Crocker found it worth while to undulate across the desert, choosing the route with the fewest obstacles, not the straightest nor shortest way. 'Give me the material I need,' he boasted, 'and I can build a mile a day of completed railroad.'

Driving the men without mercy, Crocker pushed ahead. The workers lived in dormitory boxcars three stories high, stifling hot in the arid desert. The Chinese sustained themselves with barrels of tea, washing away the alkaline dust that was proving almost as much of a menace as the snows of the Sierras. Meanwhile 2500 men shoveled to keep the

Sierra passes open so that supplies could reach the continuously moving railhead. Most equipment still had to go by way of the Horn. Providing Crocker's needs with gusto, Huntington sometimes had 30 ships loaded with rails and other supplies for the hungry Iron Horse.

Without further hitches, the rails headed for Promontory Point, the designated meeting place for the two competing iron dragons. It lay 40 miles from Ogden in Utah, just northeast of Salt Lake.

As the Central Pacific moved steadily toward that apocalyptic meeting, the Union Pacific was pushing westward from Omaha, Nebraska, just as relentlessly.

The Union Pacific had been delayed in its start for lack of working capital. By the end of 1865, only 40 miles of track had been laid. It only began to get fully underway in early 1866, thanks to some ingenious financial planning similar to Crocker's Contract & Finance Company. In this case the construction company which the railroad officials formed for themselves was called the Credit Mobilier. With its cooperation, the Union Pacific was now making up for lost time.

While Charles Crocker drove his primarily tea-drinking Chinese crew across the top of the Sierras, another man of courage drove an equally hard-working, primarily hard-drinking, Irish gang across the Rockies toward Utah. He was Grenville M Dodge, as adventurous, intelligent, lucky and determined as Theodore Judah, but like Crocker, not as fragile. He, too, was a surveyor and engineer, a man of the outdoors; in addition he was a fearless fighter whose friends included military giants such as Ulysses S Grant,

Philip Sheridan, George McClellan and William T Sherman. He commanded the respect of Thomas Durant, Union Pacific mastermind, and numbered Abraham Lincoln among his acquaintances.

Dodge was born in 1831 in Massachusetts and went to work for the railroads at an early age. When he was 20 he was offered a surveyor's job on the Illinois Central. Throwing in his lot with the railroads, he moved with the frontier which was inevitably being pushed westward by the puffing black engines. Soon he was working for Thomas Durant, Superintendent of the Rock Island Railroad, in western Illinois. Durant first filled him with his plans for a transcontinental, then sent him off to survey a route between Council Bluffs, Iowa, and the Rockies. Later, Durant and Dodge between them would do for the Union Pacific what Judah had done for the Central Pacific: they would find the route, get the permissions, and most importantly, attract the money to begin the project.

Dodge spent five years, much of it on his own time, mapping the transcontinental road. When the Civil War broke out, he joined the Army as a colonel. Only two years later he was made general. In 1864 he was sent by the Army to the western Plains to take part in the Indian Wars against the Sioux, Arapahoes, Cheyennes and others. Dodge, his eye already on future railroad routes, fought Indians and surveyed for passes at the same time. He claimed to have discovered the important Lone Tree Pass in the Laramie Mountains while being chased by angry Sioux.

His railroad friends in Washington, appreciating his prowess in the Indian Wars, exerted influence to get him

To Take Effect February 8th, 1869, at 12:05 A. M.

In Cases of Uncertainty, always take the Safe Side.

No. 3. CENTRAL PACIFIC RAILROAD. 1869.
HUMBOLDT DIVISION.

For the Government and Information of Employees only, and is not intended for the information of the Public. The Company reserves the right to vary the same as circumstances may require.

EASTWARD.						STATIONS.	WESTWARD.					
		1		**3**		**5**		**2**	**4**	**6**		
		Passenger.		Freight.		Freight.		Freight.	Passenger.	Freight.		
Distances.		3.45	AM	5.30	AM	11.00	PM	LEAVE..WINNEMUCCA..ARRIVE	3.45 PM	2.00 "	4.40		6	180
6		4.10M	"	6.00	"	11.30	"	........TULE........	3.15 "	1.35 "	4.10 M		11	174
11	17	4.55	"	6.55	"	12.30	AM	........GOLCONDA........	2.15 "	12.50 "	2.35 "		11	163
11	28	5.40	"	7.50	"	1.30 M	"	........IRON POINT........	1.10 PM	12.10 PM	1.30 M "		13	152
13	41	6.35	"	8.55	"	2.35	"	........STONEHOUSE........	12.00 "	11.15 "	12.15 AM		14	139
14	55	7.30	"	10.05 M / 10.40 M	"	3.45	"	........BATTLE MOUNTAIN........	10.40 M "	10.15 M "	11.00 "		9	125
9	64	8.05	"	11.30	"	4.35	"	........NEBUR........	9.50 "	9.40 "	10.15 "		8	116
8	72	8.35 M / 8.50 M	"	12.15 M / 12.50 M	PM	5.15 / 5.35	"	........ARGENTA........	9.00 Psd / 7.35 M "	9.05 M / 8.50 M "	9.35 "		11	108
11	83	9.30	"	1.30	"	6.25 M	"	........SHOSHONE........	6.25 M "	8.05 "	8.40 "		10	97
10	93	10.10	"	2.20	"	7.35 M	"	........BE-O-WA-WE........	5.35 "	7.30 M "	7.50 "		8	87
8	101	10.45	"	3.00	"	8.15	"	........CLURO........	4.55 "	7.00 "	7.05 "		11	79
11	112	11.25	"	4.00	"	9.15	"	........PALISADE........	4.00 "	6.20 "	6.15 "		9	68
9	121	12.00 / 12.45	PM	5.25 M / 5.55 M	PM	10.00 / 10.30	"	........CARLIN........	5.15 / 10.45 "	5.15 M "	5.35 M "		11	59
11	132	12.50	"	6.40	"	11.15	"	........MOLEEN........	9.30 "	4.55 "	3.05 "		12	48
12	144	1.40	"	7.55	"	12.30	PM	........ELKO........	8.15 "	4.10 AM	2.50 "		10	36
10	154			8.55	"	1.50 M	"	........OSINO........	7.10 "		1.50 M "		10	26
10	164			9.50	"	2.55	"	........PEKO........	6.20 "		1.00 PM		16	
16	180			11.15	"	4.30	"	ARRIVE DEETH........LEAVE	5.00 PM		11.45 AM			Distances.

If Trains are not met at the Regular Meeting Place, approach sidings carefully, until they are met.

The letter "M" set against a Station signifies a Meet—"Ps," Pass—"Psd," Passed. Meeting and Passing places are Stopping Places. Trains will arrive at Stations on time, as given in the Table, and leave as soon thereafter as business will permit.

Passenger Trains will stop at all Stations against which figures are set, except those marked †, at which they will stop to leave and on signal to take passengers. No. 1 will run daily, Mondays excepted. No. 4 will run daily, Saturdays excepted. All other trains will run daily

Attention is called to Rule No. 31.

JOHN CORNING, Ass't Gen'l Sup't.   **JAS. CAMPBELL, Div'n Sup't.**   **C. CROCKER, General Sup't.**

put in charge of a vast section of western territory (including Kansas, Wyoming, Dakota, Utah, Colorado and Montana) where, with the help of his Army friends, he efficiently proceeded to eradicate Indians. As General Sheridan explained their case to an Indian Chief: 'The only good Indian is a dead Indian.' Dodge was brutal to his enemies and callous toward his men. Finally, under pressure from some of the reform elements beginning to emerge across the nation, Washington ordered Dodge to disengage. Angrily he resigned his commission. Durant for one was happy to learn that Dodge was at liberty. He was now Vice-President of the Union Pacific where construction was stalled. His chief engineer, Peter A Dey, had resigned in an altercation over the slovenly ethics involved in the awarding of contracts, a stand by a man of integrity similar to the one which had gotten Judah in trouble with the Big Four.

Dodge accepted Durant's offer, undertaking the formidable task. Credit Mobilier head Oakes Ames put the case clearly:

'To undertake the construction of a railroad, at any price, for a distance of nearly 700 miles in a desert and unexplored country, its line crossing three mountain ranges at the highest elevations yet attempted on this continent, extending through a country swarming with hostile Indians, by whom locating engineers and conductors of construction trains were repeatedly killed and scalped at their work; upon a route destitute of water, except as supplied by watertrains, hauled from one to 150 miles, to thousands of men and animals engaged in construction; the immense mass of material, iron, ties, lumber, provisions and supplies necessary to be transported from 500 to 1500 miles – I admit might well, in the light of subsequent history and the mutations of opinion, be regarded as the freak of a madman if it did not challenge the recognition of a higher motive.'

A commanding leader, Dodge directed his men (sometimes up to 25,000 were at work at one time) as if it were war. To carry out his every order he hired General John Casement, 'the champion track-layer of the continent.' From his train Casement could 'arm a thousand men at a word; and from him, as a head, down to his chief spiker, [the crew] could be commanded by experienced officers of every rank, from general to captain.'

Dodge had men from almost every nation, including Indians, working for him. However, it was the brawny, brawling Irish that contributed most of the backbreaking work.

Across the flat lands, laying a mile of track a day was expected. Often four and five miles of track were in place by sunset. Dodge's army training lent a fierce discipline to the work. The excessive speed was largely unnecessary, its motive stockholder greed. The rival companies were not merely building the railroad, but competing for the lucrative landgrants and government loans that came with each hard-earned mile completed. The excruciating drive across the land was vividly described by an anonymous chronicler of the times:

'We, pundits of the Far East, stood upon that embankment, only about a thousand miles this side of sunset, and backed westward before that hurrying corps of sturdy operators with a mingled feeling of amusement, curiosity and profound respect. On they

California Governor George Pardee and friends bound for a fishing trip aboard the cow-catcher of a locomotive. Pardee was the Golden State's governor from 1903 to 1907.

came. A light car drawn by a single horse, gallops up to the front with its load of rails. Two men seize the end of a rail and start forward, the rest of the gang taking hold by twos, until it is clear of the car. They come forward at a run. At the word of command the rail is dropped in its place, right side up with care, while the same process goes on at the other side of the car. Less than 30 seconds to a rail for each gang, and so four rails go down to the minute. Quick work, you say, but the fellows on the Union Pacific are tremendously in earnest. The moment the car is empty it is tipped over on the side of the track to let the next loaded car pass it, and then it is tipped back again; and it is a sight to see it go flying back for another load propelled by a horse at full gallop at the end of 60 or 80 feet of rope, ridden by a young Jehu, who drives furiously. Close behind the first gang come the gaugers, spikers, and bolters, and a lively time they make of it. It is a grand "anvil chorus" that the sturdy sledges are playing across the plains. It is in triple time, three strokes to the spike. There are 10 spikes to a rail, 400 rails to a mile, 1,800 miles to San Francisco – 21 million times are those sledges to be swung; 21 million times are they to come down with their sharp punctuation before the great work of modern America is complete.'

Some 300 workers lived in a 'perpetual train' near the railhead. They slept in dormitory-like boxcars 85 feet long, beds stacked in triple tiers. They ate in almost perpetual shifts in the dining car, a long carriage with a table running down its whole length. Plates were nailed to the table to prevent loss, and a man climbed over the table to get a seat for his meal.

The diet was primarily bread, beef and coffee with good Kentucky whisky somehow always available. The meat was fresh; large herds grazed along the tracks under the supervision of contract-suppliers.

As the tracks snaked along, every 50 to 60 miles, a railroad town would appear as if a mirage in the desert. It would begin as soon as the site of a railhead was designated by the supervisors. Overnight gamblers, pimps, women, saloon-keepers, thieves and minor riff-raff – all the intricate network of ways to separate hard-earned money from the worn pockets of its owners – would move to the new location. By the time the rails arrived, the peripatetic townfolk were already tented up. Newspapers and stores were as quick as any to establish themselves in hastily put together structures, and sometimes an insubstantial hotel was ready for visitors.

Working at breakneck speed, the rough and rowdy laborers would approach the wild town, taking advantage of its tawdry delights, and then as swiftly pass it by. Overnight it would be deserted, coyotes prowling its empty streets, another railhead city some 50 miles ahead having materialized out of nowhere to take its place.

Henry M Stanley, reporting for the New York *Tribune*, described the beguiling denizens of one such town:

'These women are expensive articles, and come in for a large share of the money wasted. In broad daylight they may be seen gliding through the dusty streets carrying fancy derringers slung to their waists, with which tools they are dangerously expert. Western chivalry will not allow them to be abused by any man they may have robbed. Mostly everyone seemed bent on debauchery and dissipation.'

These tawdry towns, springing up to meet the needs of thousands, drying up as the army of workers rolled on, were known as 'hell on wheels.' For all their flashy vulgarity, they gave a measure of fun and excitement to the otherwise mind-numbing work.

The Union Pacific did not have the same problems that haunted the Central Pacific, but it had ones almost as severe. As Oakes Ames pointed out, one of the prime obstacles was Indian attacks. Workers kept their guns with them at all times, side-by-side with their Ames shovels. Surveyors, working at $60 a month, were often found scalped and mutilated. Bone-freezing cold sometimes brought work to a halt. Danger and hardship never seemed to deflect the railroad man. Only the opportunity to make more money by mining, farming, or going into business for oneself might inveigle a man from his job.

In this way the Union Pacific built 1086 miles of rail to reach Promontory, Utah. It got an estimated $74 million in return plus landgrants. The Central Pacific built 689 miles for a total of $47 million in bonds and some $64,623,512 in Federal and local landgrants. The Big Four made their money by letting contracts to their own construction company, then inflating the costs of construction and pocketing the difference. The directors and investors in the Union

Pacific managed to do the same through their 'in-group' company, the Credit Mobilier. They contracted with themselves to build at $96,000 to a mile for construction estimated to cost no more than half that amount.

This group was set up in 1864, when Abraham Lincoln called on his friend, Massachusetts Congressman Oakes Ames to ask him to see if he could somehow finance the Union Pacific Railroad. The Union Pacific, a semi-public concern chartered by Congress, was unable to proceed with construction for lack of working capital. Ames, with his brother Oliver, was a shovel manufacturer. He got together with an eccentric named, appropriately, George Francis Train, and came up with the simple plan of forming a construction company that would contract with the Union Pacific for all construction. It would be owned by the Union Pacific directors and their friends who could foresee enough immediate profit to motivate investing their capital.

The 'diamond mine,' as Ames later referred to it, was called the Credit Mobilier – the 'moving loan' company. In return for $1000, a stockholder received a $1000 bond in the Union Pacific plus an equally good $1000 share in the Credit Mobilier. In 1867, a more than satisfying dividend

Washington to testify as to their own financial structures, their records had all conveniently disappeared in a fire the month before. It was hard for them to remember the facts and figures. The close-mouthed foursome never did have a falling out.

But the scandal would not break to disillusion the country until 1872. In the spring of 1869 the people felt nothing but joy and admiration toward the railroads. Breathing fire like two giant dragons, undulating across the hot flatlands, the Union Pacific and the Central Pacific carried the dreams of a nation along with them. When there were only 16 miles between them, Charles Crocker, with his fine sense of drama, took up a challenge made to him by Thomas Durant that his men could not build 10 miles of track in a day. A wager of $10,000 was made.

Crocker prepared well. Gathering all his materials ahead of time, stacking them neatly in place, he set the men to work. There were five trains carrying the needed rails, spikes, bolts and equipment. Ten of the strongest Irish railroaders volunteered to lay the tracks. Much to the disgust of Union Pacific Chief Engineer Grenville Dodge, the ties were already in place. The work began at seven in the morning. A hand-picked crew, mostly brawny Irish, was ready to go. Twelve hours later a record 10 miles and 56 feet had been neatly spiked in place and carefully ballasted. The $10,000 was won by Crocker. His men got four extra days' pay for their incredible feat, one never since repeated. Union Pacific workers who proposed to surpass their rivals were too late. Crocker had seen to it that there were less than 10 miles to Promontory.

Day by day, as the two tracks closed the gap, newspapers reported the race with mounting excitement. The nation followed every move, entranced. Finally there was only one last mile, then on 10 May 1869, one last, highly polished, California-laurel tie standing between the Central Pacific's wood-burning *Jupiter* and the Union Pacific's coal-burning, prosaically named, *Engine Number 119*, both standing at otherwise unimportant Promontory in Utah.

About 500 dignitaries, coolies and other workers, plus hangers-on of all colorful sorts arrived in trains to mark the august occasion. As had become customary at ceremonies to honor the completion of a railroad, champagne poured forth abundantly.

There were several symbolic spikes to be lightly tapped into pre-cut holes, each one to be accompanied by a speech or two. California gave two golden spikes; Nevada sent one of Comstock silver; Arizona made one of an alloy of gold, silver and iron; Idaho and Montana offered spikes of silver and gold. These were immediately taken out and later curved into miniature spikes to be given to some few lucky company officials as souvenirs.

General Dodge, who had done so much to bring the vast endeavor to completion, described the event with evident joy:

> 'The two trains pulled up facing each other, each crowded with workmen who sought advantageous positions to witness the ceremonies, and literally covered the cars. The officers and invited guests formed on each side of the track, leaving it open to the south. The telegraph lines had been brought to that point so that in the final spiking as each blow was struck the telegraph recorded it at each connected office from the Atlantic to the Pacific. Prayer was offered.

of 100 percent was declared. Contracts sometimes paid over $340 on each $100 share. Ames did not insist that some of the lucky beneficiaries pay even minimal margins of 10 percent. He offered beguiling bonds to many highly placed Washington officials all the way up to Vice-President Schuyler Colfax and to President U S Grant's trusted secretary, Orville Babcock. As Ames later explained quite candidly, he liked to distribute his largesse, 'where it would do the most good.'

Many a respectable political reputation would be irreparably tarnished by the scandal which hit the front pages in 1872 when Durant and Ames fell out. Ames was publicly censured by a Congress which had hitherto found nothing reprehensible in taking bribes from anyone and everyone. The inescapable conclusion was that it was not the bribing, but the honest account of it that was being censured. Although seemingly slight punishment, the disgrace broke Ames, who died only a year later. None of the other initiators of the Credit Mobilier were punished.

No doubt the Big Four, who had been quietly doing the same thing with their Contract & Finance Company, found the Congressional show highly instructive. When called to

Above: On 10 May 1869 the last rails of the Union Pacific and Central Pacific were joined at Promontory, Utah. A train from the East and one from the West halted within a few feet of each other and a historic scene was then enacted. Leland Stanford drove the last gold spike (*below*), which marked the completion of the first chain of railroads to span the continental United States.

The engineers ran up their locomotives until they touched, the engineer upon each engine breaking a bottle of champagne upon the other one, and thus the two roads were welded into one great trunk line.'

Finally there was silence. Leland Stanford was given a silver hammer to hit the last golden spike. The nation listened. He missed. To avoid explanations, the telegraph operator courteously tapped the wire, and the nation

The Pacific Railroad ground broken Fany. 8th 1863, and completed May 8th 1869

exulted. Dodge went on to describe the excitement that engulfed the country, now linked as one:

'The booming of cannons and the ringing of bells were united with other species of noisemaking of which jubilant humanity finds expression for its feeling on such an occasion. The buildings in the cities were gay with flags and bunting. Business was suspended and the longest process that San Francisco had ever seen attested the enthusiasm of the people. At night the city was brilliant with illuminations. Free railway trains filled Sacramento with an unwonted crowd, and the din of cannon, steam whistles, and bells followed the final message.

At the eastern terminus of Omaha, the firing of hundreds of guns on Capitol Hill, more bells and steam whistles, and a grand procession of fire companies, civic societies, citizens and visiting delegations echoed the sentiments of the Californians. In Chicago, a procession four miles in length, a lavish display of decoration in the city and on the vessels in the river, and an address by Vice-President Colfax in the evening were the evidence of the city's feeling. In New York by order of the mayor, a salute of 100 guns announced culmination of the great undertaking.

In other large cities of the country the expressions of public gratification were hardly less hearty and demonstrative.'

Dodge had reason to be proud. And in the meantime, opportunities for new endeavors danced like sugar plums in everyone's heads. With railroads, what was not possible?

By Rail Across the Wild West

'They reclined in luxury upon the easy-cushioned, revolving chairs; they surveyed with infinite satisfaction the elegance of the fly-parlor in which they sat. They said that none but Americans or enchanted princes in the Arabian Nights ever traveled in such state. But the general appearance of the passengers hardly suggested greater wealth than elsewhere; and they were plainly in that car because they were of the American race, which finds nothing too good for it that its money can buy.'

William Dean Howells was commenting on the journey of the ages, the early rides across the continent on the newly-completed transcontinental railroad. In the first year of operation some 150,000 passengers jostled for seats. Within another 12 years, the number would have swollen to one million. First-class passengers traveled for $100, second-class travelers paid $80 for a much less comfortable privilege.

During the next thirty years, four more transcontinentals would be built: Josiah Perham's Northern Pacific completed in 1883; the Big Four's Southern Pacific, also completed in 1883; Cyrus Kurtz Holliday's Atchison, Topeka & Santa Fe, finished in 1885; and finally James J Hill's Great Northern, the last of the great transcontinentals, built after the land-grant give-away had been stopped, and completed in 1893. These transcontinental trunklines, with their spurs to enterprising towns and districts, served to open the Northwest and Southwest to ever-increasing numbers of visitors and settlers. By 1900, some 70,000 miles of steel crisscrossed the no-longer Wild West. The nineteenth century would see the nation, which had already been patched together by the outcome of the Civil War, bound indissolubly by its railroads.

Once the first transcontinental was finished, what desire there was to cross over that frail iron track! By then rail travel in the East had become fairly expert; the telegraph was in use to guide trains, serving to prevent head-on collisions; Pullman had built his palatial cars, making travel by rail more luxurious than any other type of travel; and railroad companies had already begun to bring immigrants by the carload to their land-grant sections of the plains and prairies.

As soon as the two engines bumped cowcatchers that cold clear morning at Promontory Point, people came from all over the world to view the wonders of the extra-

Below: The Oregon Express stands outside the Central Pacific station at Sacramento in about 1882. The photograph was taken looking west at the back of the station, from the old trestle across China Slough. Later, freight trains passed to the left of the station in order to get on the new bridge, which was replaced in 1930.

ordinary Wild West. The rich and the poor, the settler and the visitor, speaking their many languages, bringing their many gifts, each came to change and form the young nation. For the West was not a firmly defined culture. In the beginning, newcomers were not required to fit into a pre-existing pattern but were constantly contributing, with their own idiosyncracies and know-how, to the creation of the culture of the West.

On one early transcontinental visit, the French writer Louis Laurent Simonin noted the wonderful mix of peoples he came across wherever he traveled: 'The Spaniard Dominguez, married to a Frenchwoman; the mine captains from English Cornwall, the prospectors, the exploiters of lodes, Irish, Germans, Italians, Canadians, French – each with the distinctive characteristics of his race, and all with the common traits of persistence, energy, coolness.' Within the next 30 years some six million persistent people would pour onto American shores and many of these flooded into the far West.

For chroniclers it was the adventure their readers wished most to hear about. The West had already become part of the imagination of the world. As one Englishman haughtily explained: 'A tour through the domains of Uncle Samuel without visiting the wide regions of the Far West, would be like seeing *Hamlet* with the part of the Prince of Denmark omitted.'

The journey varied greatly for each passenger but there was always the unifying experience of wonder and amazement at the awe-inspiring railroad journey. Whether one traveled to the wild West from Chicago or Omaha, St Louis, Kansas City or Duluth, it always began in the hustling and bustling chaos of a railroad station. One of the earliest chroniclers to report on such a journey, W F Rae, describes a familiar scene:

'Confusion reigns supreme here, as at most American railway stations. Excited passengers are rushing about in quest of the luggage which, despite the system of "checking" is often going astray or getting out of sight. Frantic efforts

Top: Leland Stanford's special car was built at the Central Pacific Railroad Car Works in Sacramento by Benjamin Welch, master car builder.

Above: Fireman William Buckley and Engineer George Kingsley pose with Agent Carson and Conductor Probert beside the first passenger train into Minnewaukon, North Dakota on 10 August 1885.

Below: The Atchison, Topeka & Santa Fe Railroad line unloads lumber and other freight for shipment to distant ports.

are made to attract the attention of the baggage clerk, and to induce him to attach the necessary check to the trunk or portmanteau, which has at length been discovered. Those who get this part of their business over proceed to the office in order to secure berths in Pullman's sleeping car.'

The same frantic confusion reigned for those who had not had the foresight to telegraph ahead for sleeping accommodations. To ride Pullman was to ride like a king. George M Pullman had created his cars and achieved early on a virtual monopoly over the new industry which he had formed. His cars cost some $25,000 to build and spared no expense in creating the illusion of luxury. First and foremost were springs to obviate the jolts that a hastily built roadbed offered. Then there were the plush swiveling armchairs to recline in, the stowaway bunks to sleep on, conveniences like lounges, barbers, dining cars, card tables, even organs. The decisive factor in a man getting the coveted position of conductor might be if he could play the organ.

Everything in a Pullman car was decorated in the very finest materials, from the heavy brocades to the plush, thick rugs. Chandeliers gracefully lit the opulent interiors, shining their light on exquisite marquetry that Pullman spared no expense to get. His cars, inside and out, were works of art. As his brochure explained, referring to the observation car, 'Isabella,' 'this car is 70 feet long; is heated with steam and lighted with electricity, with beautiful fixtures; the section part of the car is finished in vermillion wood, and the observation room in mahogany, elaborately designed and carved.' Some had luxurious, specially designed barber chairs. One had a stained-glass dome of exquisite Moorish-style design.

The elegant mirrors, handsome desks upon which to write careful journals, the detailing of the wood panelling, the softness of the bed-linen, all tended to make even the most fastidious feel comfortable. Everything was done with an eye for detail by the very best of craftsmen.

The railroads lost money on dining cars as a usual matter, but figured they attracted passengers. In the Pullman dining car, sumptuous repasts were served daily in dining rooms with table linen, candlelight (in the evening) and silver servings. Fresh trout from the streams and antelope steak from the prairies were succulent treats to break the monotony of the long crossing. With Pullman's attention to detail, the ride was smooth as a glide on ice; a passenger could drink his Kentucky bourbon without a jostle or a spill.

For those who could not afford the Pullman ticket, things were not quite as comfortable, although still just as interesting. Robert Louis Stevenson, in *Across the Plains*, described his journey as an 'amateur emigrant' on an American train as being somewhat of a personal experience:

'It was about two in the afternoon of Friday that I found myself with more than a hundred others, to be sorted and boxed for the journey. A white-haired official, with a stick under one arm, and a list in the other hand, stood apart in front of us, and called name after name in the tone of a command. At each name you would see a family gather up its brats and bundles and run for the hindmost of the three cars that stood awaiting us. The second car was devoted to men traveling alone, and the third to the Chinese.

The families once housed, we men carried the second car without ceremony by simultaneous assault. I suppose the reader has some notion of an American

Above: Union Pacific's locomotive No 5, hauling the photograph car, stops near Point of Rocks, Wyoming for a photograph in 1868. Construction of the transcontinental railroad was not completed until the next year, and photographers recorded scenic shots and progress along the line.

railroad car, that long, narrow wooden box, like a flat-roofed Noah's ark, with a stove and a convenience, one at either end, a passage down the middle, and transverse benches upon either hand. Those destined for emigrants on the Union Pacific are only remarkable for their extreme plainness, nothing but wood entering in any part into their constitution, and for the usual inefficacy of the lamps, which often went out and shed but a dying glimmer even while they burned.

The benches are too short for anything but a young child. Where there is scarce elbow-room for two to sit, there will not be space enough for one to lie. Hence the company's servants have conceived a plan for the better accommodation of travelers. They prevail on every two to chum together. To each of the chums they sell a board and three square cushions stuffed with straw, and covered with thin cotton. The benches can be made to face each other in pairs, for the backs are reversible. On approach of night the boards are laid from bench to bench, making a couch wide enough for two, and long enough for a man of the middle height; and the chums lie down side by side upon the cushions with the head to the conductor's van and the feet to the engine.'

If three persons got together they could share expenses for some of the amenities that make life civilized. For instance, enterprising partners might buy and share a brick of soap, a washing-dish, and a towel. Stevenson explains how this worked: 'The partners used these instruments, one after another, according to the order of their first

awaking; and when the firm had finished there was no want of borrowers. Each filled the tin dish at the water filter opposite the stove, and retired with the whole stock in trade to the platform of the car. There he knelt down, supporting himself by a shoulder against the woodwork, or one elbow crooked about the railing, and made ashift to wash his face and neck and hands; a cold, an insufficient, and, if the train is moving rapidly, a somewhat dangerous toilet.'

The West was still a glowing attraction, even to those who could not afford to travel in Pullman luxury. Albert Deane Richardson, a reporter for Horace Greeley's famous newspaper the *Tribune*, writing about the western paradise, enthuses: 'No other country on the globe equals ours beyond the Mississippi River. Its mines, forests and prairies await the capitalist. Its society welcomes the immigrant, offering high interest upon his investment of money, brains or skill; and if need be, generous obliviousness of errors past – a clean page to begin anew the record of his life. . . . We seem on the threshold of a destiny higher and better than any nation has yet fulfilled. And the great West is to rule us.'

For a long time the railroads did not seem very respectful of their new 'rulers.' Without compunction they shunted the emigrant aside, without explanation leaving passengers to broil in the sun, or freeze in the cold. Often emigrants were unceremoniously dumped out onto some tiny depot station without a town in sight, there left to wait, sometimes all night, sometimes without shelter in freezing rain, until the railroads in their infinite wisdom saw fit to pick them up again.

The adventurous well-to-do, the less affluent second-class and the tense and hopeful emigrants were not the only passengers. There were also those unkempt, clear-eyed wandering outcasts called 'hoboes.' Stevenson's first en-

Above: A photographer recorded the arrival of the first train over the Missouri River on tracks laid on ice in March 1879.

Below: Central Pacific locomotive No 82, built by Rogers in 1868, was photographed in 1890. Four-wheel 15-foot 'dinky' cabooses, like the one shown here, were in operation on the Central Pacific and Southern Pacific lines for a number of years. The cord wood piled in the tender is ready to be used for fuel.

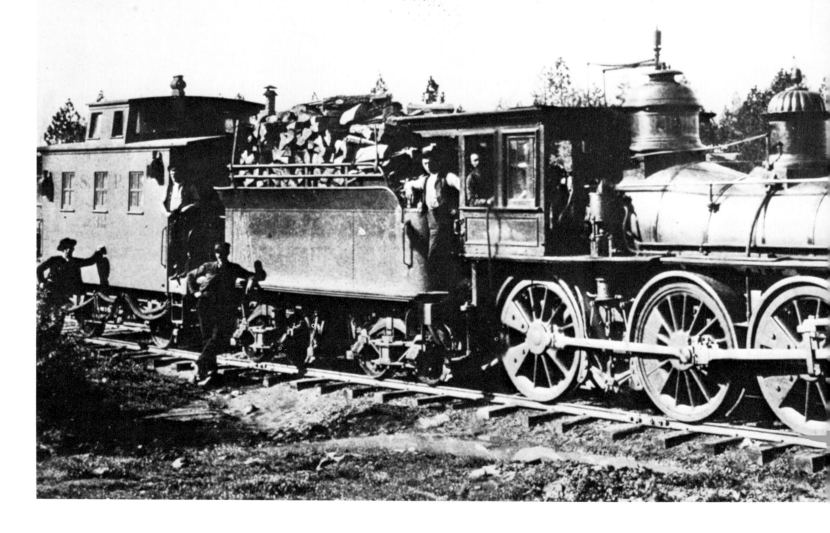

counter with these itinerant legends was less than glamorous: 'At a place called Creston, a drunken man got in. He was aggressively friendly. . . . Just as we were beginning to move out of the next station . . . by came the conductor. There was a word or two of talk; and then the official had the man by the shoulders, twitched him from his seat, marched him through the car, and sent him flying on to the track. It was done in three motions, as exact as a piece of drill. The train was still moving slowly, although beginning to mend her pace, and the drunkard got his feet without a fall. He carried a red bundle, though not so red as his cheeks; and he shook this menacingly in the air with one hand, while the other stole behind him to the region of the kidneys. It was the first indication that I had come among revolvers, and I observed it with some emotion. The conductor stood on the steps with one hand on his hip, looking back at him; and perhaps this attitude imposed upon the creature, for he turned without further ado, and went off staggering along the track towards Cromwell, followed by a peal of laughter from the cars. They were speaking English all about me, but I knew I was in a foreign land.'

This hobo was lucky that the train was moving slowly. Many railroad 'bulls' had no compunction in throwing a stowaway off a fast-moving 'varnish' (as passenger cars were called because so much varnish was used to make them shine), leaving him dead or half-dead many miles from help.

The life of the hobo was fraught with danger. Hopping trains presented the constant threat of injury. To avoid hostile railroad men, the hobo might have to lie under the cars or on top, subject to freezing cold or broiling heat. In times of depression, there were so many hoboes that the railroads made every effort to discourage them. Small skirmishes were constant, although some hoboes, like 'Springfield Mike' Rolland, might actually be in a position to save a train. Rolland had noted some loose tracks where he was walking and ran ahead far enough to stop the on-rushing express by waving his red bandana, a characteristic feature of the hobo's attire. Hoboes helped each other, too. They saw each other safely in and out of freight cars, left notes on telegraph poles, rendezvoused for their famous mulligan stew (to which a 'stiff' had to contribute something before he could partake of the ambrosial creation) at camps near railroads, and created a comforting sub-culture for the lonely men who, unable to compete in the ever-more harshly competitive world, had chosen what seems to an outsider to be the incessant struggle of the unsettled. In the 1890s it has been estimated that some 60,000 tramps were picking up occasional work on railroad sections and farms, in factories and mines, endangering life and limb, while, like leaves in an autumn wind, they blew about the countryside 'riding the rails.'

Few people, if they had their choice, however, would have chosen mulligan stew over railroad fare. For a dollar a passenger could enjoy his dinner from a menu consisting of turkey, steak, short ribs of beef, duck with jelly, salmon with anchovy sauce, mutton, chicken croquettes, vegetables, pastries, desserts, and cheeses. An ample supply of excellent wines complemented the delicious fare. With that, or any part of it, under the belt, the fate of no unfortunate hobo was going to dampen the spirits of hearty transcontinental passengers.

If a traveler did not have access to the dining car, he picnicked at his seat, or took part in the hectic meal stops at rail depots dotted along the tracks where people came from miles around to sell their wares and to watch the trains steam in and out. But no matter what glamorous dreams the locals invested in the arrivals, for the passengers these stops were at best unsatisfactory. Passengers were subject to indigestion caused by the considerable rush to get their meals. Characteristically the stop never lasted more than a half hour, and sometimes no more than ten minutes. A dishonest entrepreneur might delay long enough so that the hungry traveler had to leave before the paid-for food arrived. However, dishonesty in the early days of the West was the exception, not the rule and meals were generally greasy but good and hearty.

In 1876 Frederick Henry Harvey started an excellent railroad restaurant in Topeka, Kansas, and the idea was so novel and so appealing that he eventually had 47 comforting stops, plus 15 hotels along the Atchison, Topeka & Santa Fe line. His famous 'Harvey girls' were young women of good repute who lived in dormitories, chaperoned by a Harvey-employed matron who made sure their good character remained intact by seeing they obeyed a 10 o'clock curfew.

Above: Currier and Ives *Lightning Express* trains *Leaving the Junction.*

Another and more friendly way of sharing mealtimes was warmly reported by Stevenson: 'Before the sun was up, the stove would be brightly burning; at the first station the natives would come on board with milk and eggs and coffee cakes; and soon from end to end the car would be filled with little parties breakfasting upon the bed boards. It was the pleasantest hour of the day.'

One characteristic of the American which almost all visitors commented upon was rudeness. The courtesy the foreigner was used to in his class-conscious land was too often missing in the American West. Protecting their newly discovered freedom, people often expressed themselves roughly, forgetting the 'Sorry, sirs' and 'Thank-you-ma'ams' of their former lower positions. In like manner, the unaccustomed equality tended to instigate an aggressive 'I'm as good as you are' swagger which many visitors took for rudeness. As Frederick Trench Townshend put the case: 'The assumption of the slightest tone of superiority or command is immediately resented by a display of obstinacy, sulkiness, or insolence.'

In effect, foreigners could not patronize Americans with impunity. On the other hand, 'equality,' as Stevenson drily noted, 'though conceived largely in America, does not extend so low down as to an emigrant. Thus in all other trains, a warning cry of "All aboard!" recalls the passengers to take their seats; but as soon as I was alone with emigrants, and from the transfer all the way to San Francisco, I found this ceremony was [omitted].'

When a transfer was made from the Union Pacific Railroad company to the Central Pacific, the Pullman passengers found themselves unceremoniously pushed off the clouds of luxury that they had become accustomed to.

However, for the less affluent, the change was for the better. After several days cooped up together in less than comfortable surroundings, some of the cars had begun to smell. Fresh ones were more than welcome. As Stevenson reported: 'The cars on the Central Pacific were nearly twice as high, and so proportionally airier; they were freshly varnished, which gave us all a sense of cleanliness as though we had bathed; the seats drew out and joined in the centre, so that there was no more need for bed boards.'

All the while that physical comfort or discomfort of the train travelers was being catered to, what was it they saw when sitting still and looking out from their train windows upon the passing scene? What was the West like that had drawn so many different people from so many distant shores?

If the journey began from Chicago, five hours out the traveler traversed the Mississippi River on a bridge that was just a puckering foretaste of the spidery structures the heavy engines would dare to cross further west in the Rockies and the Sierras. W F Rae held his breath as he looked about him: 'This bridge is nearly a mile in length, and is constructed partly of wood and partly of iron. The structure has a very unsubstantial appearance, and as it creaks and sways while the train passes over it, the contingency of an unwelcome descent into the deep and rapid stream beneath is one which flashes over the mind.' And well it might, for accidents were a fairly common occurrence, the railroads deeming safeguards an infringement on their inalienable right to conduct business in any manner they saw fit.

Above: An early steam train in *The Great West.*

Omaha was the true gateway to the West on the first transcontinentals. That was where the Union Pacific began its journey. 'As mile after mile is left behind,' one journalist recorded, 'the remark is very generally made that the surrounding country, instead of being wild and desolate, is rich and filled with settlers. Farm houses and tilled fields are seen on both sides of the line, and this spectacle is a common one throughout a large tract of the State of Nebraska.'

It would not remain so appealing. Up to the ninety-eighth meridian, which more or less cuts down through the middle of Nebraska, the loam was black and rich, making farming a relatively rewarding activity. As this fertile land was swiftly settled, for just one brief moment it appeared as if the early American dream – of small independent farms stretching side by side from coast to coast – was likely to be fulfilled.

However, the train traveler soon saw that further west, in the region known as the High Plains, the land became hard with the tangled roots of bunch grass; and, although extremely fertile, it lacked sufficient water for successful small-scale farming. Incessantly blown by a mind-numbing wind, the flatlands were exposed to the additional hazards of being denuded by grasshoppers or blighted by prairie fire.

Grasshoppers would make the tracks slippery, preventing the engine's climb over even slight hills. The railroads overcame the problem through the invention of a form of automatic sand bucket. A prairie fire was another story. Many a train engineer would race a miles-wide raging inferno of a fire in an attempt to save the lives of his passengers and warn any towns lying in the path of the fiery wall. The fires,

started by lightning or carelessness, were sometimes so fierce they consumed the very soil, leaving behind only calcined material. Sometimes a new immigrant would arrive at this blackened desolation to be told it was his new homestead.

One woman remembered her arrival on the land she was about to settle: 'I shall never forget the black prairie as I saw it in 1872, just after a prairie fire had swept over it. To me, coming from southern Michigan with her clover fields, large houses and larger barns, trees, hills, and running streams, the vast stretches of black prairie never ending – no north, south, east, or west – dotted over with tiny unpainted houses – no I can't say barns – but shacks for a cow, and perhaps a yoke of oxen – that picture struck such a homesick feeling in my soul it took years to efface.'

For many miles along the south bank of the Platte River, which the first continental railroad followed across Nebraska, ran the old Emigrant Trail. Sometimes a small train of covered wagons might still be passed, reminding travelers of the precarious time when wagons were the only means used by the intrepid settlers to find their way to the West. A train of wagons, each with its team of eight or ten oxen, might stretch as far as the eye could see. Sometimes these 'Prairie Schooners' would proceed side by side so as not to be in each other's dust. Then 'the trip took as many months as it now takes days, and was seldom accomplished without the loss of several cattle, and of a few human lives.'

Many writers have recorded the golden age of America's 'golden west.' Sometimes it seems these writers had as much to do with the creation of the legend as with recording it. Bret Harte was one who introduced a memorable if roughhewn bunch of characters to the wide-eyed world,

Above: A carful of curious and somewhat anxious passengers concentrate in awe on the photographer during an early train journey across the West.

Below: Union Pacific's locomotive No 768 was built by Rogers of Paterson, New Jersey in 1887 and was photographed while still new.

Opposite top: Assorted work crew members, in a variety of occupational dress surround *Goliah* at Wadsworth, Nevada in 1880. The locomotive was built in 1867 and broken up in 1905.

Its days of glory well in the past, an old 2-6-2 steam engine rusts away undisturbed in a railroad siding in Oregon.

characters that the average visitor would look for in vain. O Henry was another who spun golden yarns about the uncouth, the no-good, and the outlaw of the Wild West, to weave them into the tapestry of world legend.

For all their power, however, few can match the vivid, tongue-in-cheek effrontery of the irrepressible Mark Twain. Twain spent several years in the West, which he catches with unerring accuracy in his descriptions such as those collected in *Roughing It*. He begins by describing an Overland Trail journey by stage, which followed the same route the railroad would later take.

'So we flew along all day. At 2 PM the belt of timber that fringes the North Platte and marks its windings through the vast level floor of the Plains came in sight. At 4 PM we crossed a branch of the river, and at 5 PM we crossed the Platte itself, and landed at Fort Kearney, 56 hours out from St Joe – 300 miles!'

Twain then goes on to quote what he purports to be a contemporary account of a railroad trip over the same ground which, he says, appeared in *The New York Times*:

'At 4:20 PM, Sunday, we rolled out of the station at Omaha, and started westward on our long jaunt. A couple of hours out, dinner was announced – an "event" to those of us who had yet to experience what

Left: A hardworking crew pauses for the photographer outside the Sacramento shops in 1889.

Below: A temporary track is laid through the town of Auburn, California, to carry a contractor's locomotive and flat cars, including a steam shovel.

it is to eat in one of Pullman's hotels on wheels; so, stepping into the car next forward of our sleeping palace, we found ourselves in the dining car. It was a revelation to us, that first dinner on Sunday. And though we continued to dine for four days, and had as many breakfasts and suppers, our whole party never ceased to admire the perfection of the arrangements, and the marvelous results achieved. Upon tables covered with snowy linen, and garnished with services of solid silver, Ethiop waiters, flitting about in spotless white, placed as by magic a repast at which Delmonico himself could have had no occasion to blush; and, indeed, in some respects it would be hard for that distinguished *chef* to match our *menu*; for, in addition to all that ordinarily makes up a first-chop dinner, had we not our antelope steak (the gormand who has not experienced this – bah! what does he know of the feast of fat things?), our delicious mountain-brook trout, and choice fruits and berries, and (sauce piquant and unpurchasable!) our sweet-scented, appetite-compelling air of the prairies? You may depend upon it, we all did justice to the good things, and as we washed them down with bumpers of sparkling Krug, whilst we sped along at the rate of 30 miles an hour, agreed it was the fastest living we had ever experienced. (We beat that, however, two days afterward when we made *twenty-seven miles in twenty-seven minutes*, while our champagne glasses filled to the brim spilled not a drop!)

After dinner we repaired to our drawing room car, and, as it was Sabbath eve, intoned some of the grand hymns – "Praise God from," etc.; "Shining Shore," "Coronation," etc. – the voices of the men singers and of the women singers blending sweetly in the evening air, while our train, with its great, glaring Polyphemus eye, lighting up long vistas of prairie, rushed into the night and the Wild. Then to bed in luxurious couches, where we slept the sleep of the just and only awoke the next morning (Monday) at eight o'clock to find ourselves at the crossing of the North Platte, 300 miles from Omaha – *fifteen hours and forty minutes out*.'

People came to the West with widely varied preconceptions, prejudices, and deeply-felt hopes. All of them shared a profound curiosity about the Indians. By the time the railroad puffed across the continent, many of the tribes had been killed off, or had been relegated to unproductive reservation land, their spirits broken, their opportunities unconscionably curtailed. As William T Sherman prophesied, '10,000 tracklayers will bring in with them enough whisky to kill every Indian within a hundred miles.' But some Indians would continue to war on for another 25 years. They continued to derail trains, scalp and torture settlers, bravely fight soldiers bent on their destruction and sometimes seek a means of accommodation with the whites. They also came pathetically to the stations begging for pennies. They took part in circuses and rodeos, behaving with the mute and mournful dignity of captured animals.

Some railroads offered free transportation to the tribes living along the tracks, segregating them into uncomfortable box-like cars. Their chiefs were allowed to sit in among the regular passengers. This custom had had a modifying effect on a few of the tribes, as some braves tended to forgo derailing an engine and scalping its passengers in favor of a thrilling ride on the Iron Horse.

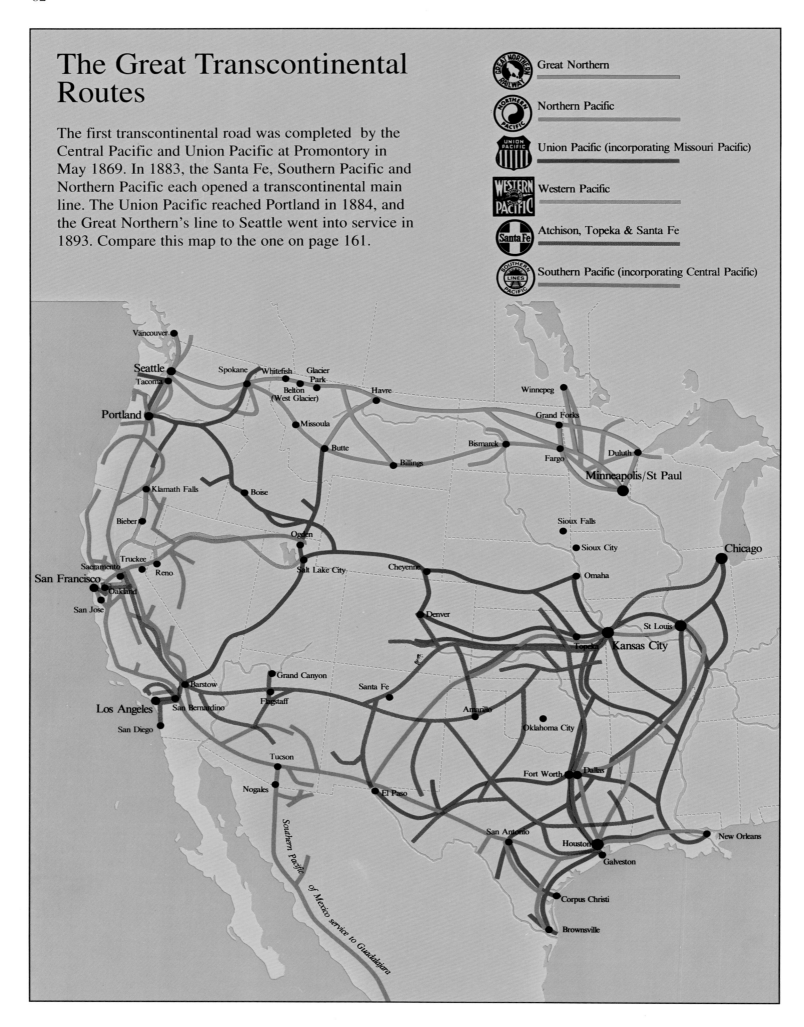

The Great Transcontinental Routes

The first transcontinental road was completed by the Central Pacific and Union Pacific at Promontory in May 1869. In 1883, the Santa Fe, Southern Pacific and Northern Pacific each opened a transcontinental main line. The Union Pacific reached Portland in 1884, and the Great Northern's line to Seattle went into service in 1893. Compare this map to the one on page 161.

Great Northern

Northern Pacific

Union Pacific (incorporating Missouri Pacific)

Western Pacific

Atchison, Topeka & Santa Fe

Southern Pacific (incorporating Central Pacific)

Filled as they were with horror stories about Indian atrocities, the whites were not sympathetic to the individuals they encountered, as the diarist Grace Greenwood demonstrates sourly: 'Just out of the town we saw a freight train partially loaded with a hideous cargo – a lot of dirty, lazy, greasy-looking Indians and squaws – and at one of the stations where we stopped for water we encountered a tall Pawnee, in a flaming red shirt and a peculiarly airy fashion of "breeks," that garment being slashed, with nothing inserted in the slashes, and with several pendant portions fluttering in the evening breeze. His hair was arranged in three long chatelaine braids, hanging gracefully down his back. He was a "pashaw of Three Tails," not counting the before-mentioned tags of drapery. He announced himself as a physician, and, with savage ingenuousness and love of symbols, he carried a bow and arrows. . . . These native gentlemen give a wild flavor to the scene, but on the whole I think I prefer the antelopes and the prairie-dog.'

Miss Greenwood went on her mincing way, while nobler souls sought to record with greater compassion the Indians' plight. The painters Alfred Miller and George Catlin lived with the tribes, sometimes painting Indian men and women in all their extravagant formality, and as often in their harsh and dangerous everyday tasks. Thomas Moran and Alfred Bierstadt sought to bring onto their small canvasses the grandeur of the western mountain scenery that had been home to the Indian – no small effort, but they succeeded in no small measure.

The most ambitious painter and sculptor of all to record the passing of the West was Frederick Remington. Ranging the gamut of the West, Remington captured the life of the hardy, rowdy cowboys, the brave and beleaguered Indians, the well-disciplined, courageous Army. In all, he painted 2739 pictures about his beloved West, and illustrated 147 books, eight of which he had written himself. He not only preserved, but did much to create the legend of that golden age.

Loving every minute of his life in the wide open spaces, he made friends with most of the people he met, including Theodore Roosevelt, whom he later followed to Cuba and painted charging up San Juan Hill. One friend tried to explain Remington's eager embrace of an unaccustomedly rugged life, saying he was just a 'big, goodnatured, overgrown boy.'

But Remington was more sensitive than his exuberance might have suggested. Not long after he arrived from the East, and earlier than most, Remington noted the evanascent nature of the Wild West. Years later he could still remember the day when he was sitting on a hill watching a train chug across the seemingly infinite prairie: 'I knew the wild riders and the vacant land were about to vanish forever, and the more I considered the subject, the bigger the Forever loomed.'

When the first travelers crossed the continent behind one of those engines, which Remington noted were drawing destruction like a Pullman diner in its train, they were struck most forcibly by the open sky, the boundless horizon, the emptiness of the earth. 'Immense,' 'immeasurable,' 'vast' are adjectives that recur over and over in the journals of the time.

A good deal of prime agricultural acreage was turned over to ranchers because they lacked water for farming. The quarter sections offered free to settlers by the generous Federal Homestead Act of 1862 were soon in the hands of

This defunct Vancouver, Seattle and Portland locomotive has been boarded up and put to rest in a railroad siding in Oregon.

large ranch owners whose holdings extended for thousands of acres. The quarter section, which had seemed so adequate when applied to the rich lands east of the ninety-eighth meridian, was far too small for most farm enterprises which, like the ranches, would have to grow large in order to offset the ferocious cycles of drought and plenty.

The cattle industry flourished under the impact of the railroads, following the railheads as they dug into the remoter regions of the West. After the Civil War many veterans went off to Texas and found thousands of the tough but fat Texas longhorns freely wandering the range for the taking. It was the beginning of a new industry.

In *A Scamper through America or, Fifteen Thousand Miles of Ocean and Continent in Sixty Days*, T S Hudson wrote wonderingly of the cattle he saw fattening on this remarkable land: 'A herd of 5000 head will feed the year round and grow fat on a stretch of arid-looking table-land, where an English farmer, if he saw it in the autumn, would vow there was not sufficient grazing for his children's donkey.' Many young Englishmen went west to take up ranching in the 1870s, accounting for one in three ranchers in Colorado alone. They learned the ways of the cowboys, delighting in the fact that one man could handle a thousand rambunctious animals by himself.

The flatness that visitors found either entrancing or appalling about the prairies and high plains made problems for homesteaders. There was so little wood that people built what were called sod houses. These were either dug down into the earth and covered over with thick prairie sod, known colloquially as 'Prairie marble,' or built up by using sod squares like bricks. It was better to dig down, however, since it gave additional protection from the winter's bone-chilling wind.

There being few towns in this part of the West, settlers arrived at their new homes to begin their lives alone. The support system offered by a town, its cultural amenities, its opportunities for friendships, its markets for trade, were for a long time lacking on the prairies. The homesteader and his family made a valiant, if lonely, struggle. The men did not mind so much, bent as they were on their new project, relishing their newfound independence. The women often went mad.

Towns did follow the railroads, as did so much else in western America. Cheyenne, Laramie, Abilene, Dodge, Ellsworth became famous for their extravagant ways. Denver sprang from nothing to a thriving city in less than three years, soon boasting an opera house and three theaters and a church. Richardson enthused over Nevada's

Above: A stage coach of the old 'Pioneer Line' meets a Southern Pacific passenger train outside the Wells Fargo Express depot.

silver-mining center, Virginia City: 'Here has sprung up like Jonah's gourd upon a hill, which cannot be hid; a city of costly churches, tasteful school-houses, and imposing hotels; many telegraph wires, many daily coaches, two theaters, three daily newspapers – one nearly as large as the eight-page journals of New York! But five years past, a desert – today a metropolis!'

Colorado became known as 'England beyond the Missouri' because of the prevalence of its visitors from that land. One Earl of Dunraven helped to build an excellent hotel there, called the English Hotel. This did much to enhance travel because staying in some hotels was less than satisfying, as one Charles Messiter explained, telling of an overnight stay in Cheyenne. The hotel 'contained only one room for men, in which there were 27 beds, each meant for two. You never knew who you were going to have as a companion – very frequently a half-drunken wagon-driver, who before he got into bed deposited a loaded revolver under the pillow.'

The air in Colorado, as might be expected, drew praise from all visitors. The writer William Baillie-Grohman stated that it was 'dry and sparkling as perhaps none other on the globe. It seems to be composed not of one-fifth, but of five-fifths of oxygen. You feel that it is air which has never before been breathed.'

The Frenchman Louis Laurent Simonin – getting in the bragadoccio spirit of the West – said of Cheyenne, after hearing it might become a part of Colorado: 'this little city does not want to be annexed to Colorado, it wants to annex Colorado. It does not even wish to be a part of Dakota. It dreams of detaching a fragment from this territory and from Colorado and Utah, which it will call Wyoming, and of which it will be the center. So is local patriotism born.'

'A few years ago,' explained another scribe exploring the Southwest, 'one would have said that San Antonio was enjoying a boom. But you cannot use that expression now, for the western men have heard that a boom, no matter how quickly it rises, often comes down just as quickly, and so forcibly that it makes a hole in the ground where castles

in the air had formerly stood. So if you wish to please a western man by speaking well of his city (and you cannot please him more in any other way), you must say that it is enjoying a "steady, healthy growth." San Antonio is enjoying a steady, healthy growth.'

That was the best you might say about towns for some time after the 'hell-on-wheels' and later the hell-raising cattle towns were tamed by the arrival of law-abiding settlers. At which point some reported, as Isabella Bird did about Denver, that life in the West 'is a moral, hard, unloving, unrelieved, unbeautified, grinding life.' Writers who had spent their youth in some of these cultural deserts would grow up to excoriate the dullness and small-mindedness of these steadily spreading towns with even greater passion.

Visitors were not always bent on settling or reporting. Some came merely for fun. In 1874 Windham Thomas Wyndham-Quin, the fourth Earl of Dunraven and Mountearl, visited Colorado where he had ranchland (and would later build his hotel). He wrote in a book called *The Great Divide*: 'Having two or three months of spare time, I determined to pay a visit to the far-famed region of the Upper Yellowstone, and to judge for myself whether the thermal springs and geysers there situated were deserving of the superiority claimed for them.' He set off on an adventure with a local guide, a rancher friend, his own artist, a personal physician, a Scottish gunbearer, a servant and his dog Tweed.

Although protected by his entourage, Dunraven was surprised that adventure escaped him. 'I never have an adventure worth a cent,' he wrote. 'Nobody ever scalps me; I don't get jumped by highwaymen. It never occurs to a bear to hug me, and my very appearance inspires feelings of dismay or disgust in the breast of the puma or mountain lion. It is true that I have often been horribly frightened, but generally without any adequate cause.'

Another flamboyant visitor was Grand Duke Alexis of Russia, who came with an entourage of 500, and had as his guides no lesser hunters than General Philip Sheridan and Colonel George A Custer. Alexis was the son of the Czar of Russia and was bent on bagging the supreme prize of a hunt in the Wild West, the peaceful buffalo. The persistent Grand Duke's party managed to bag 200 in one day. Reported a newspaper: 'The Grand Duke has killed the first horned monster, and reached the apex of American excitement.'

As a matter of fact the Grand Duke was barely in time. Within two years of his visit in 1871, the buffalo would be close to extinction, thousands of carcasses rotting on the plains. The buffalo had been the economic basis for Indian culture. The animal provided meat, clothes, and tents for his survival. The Indian picked off the buffalo in a symbiotic arrangement that threatened neither group. When the first white men arrived on the Great Plains, the vast herds, estimated at some 12 million animals, covered Kansas and Texas territory sometimes as far as the eye could see.

Colorful 'Buffalo Bill' Cody was the prime hunter in the last days of the herds. He led the big game hunters who hung their trophies on the platforms of their private trains. Many people had their own personal hunting cars, and traveled for months in such luxury that even passengers in the famous Pullman's were made to look as if they were roughing it.

Cody also led Wild West tours where people could indiscriminately shoot into the herds nosing curiously around the trains. Professional hide-hunters and unprofessional bounty-hunters bent on getting their three dollars a hide abetted the extinction of the magnificent beasts. The railroads concurred because the herds wrecked tracks and sometimes knocked over an engine. A train might be delayed several hours while a peaceful herd crossed its path. The Army winked at the butchery, figuring it would help keep the Indians on their reservations.

Richard Dodge describes the carnage he saw in 1873: 'Where there were myriads of buffalo the year before, there

Above: This perky little locomotive, the first in the Northwest on the St Paul & Pacific Railroad, which was the predecessor of the Great Northern, arrived in St Paul on a steamboat in 1861.

Below: In the early days western railroads used water spouting devices on locomotives to chase buffalo off the tracks.

were now myriads of carcasses. The air was foul with sickening stench, and the vast plain, which only a short twelve months before teemed with animal life, was a dead, solitary putrid desert.' Hunting the buffalo for fun was one more nineteenth-century folly.

No matter how many delays on the punishing prairie, when the train finally reached the mountains, westbound passengers began to experience the greatest excitement of their journey. If it were winter, snowdrifts might impede passage for hours at a time. If spring, a bridge might be washed out. The bridges, flimsy trestle spans across mind-boggling ravines, were never completely secure. Sometimes a cautious engineer might uncouple his engine and bravely take it across without passenger cars. If the bridge stood, he would come back and draw his train along. The process was never reassuring. Accidents were not infrequent as engines sometimes jumped the tracks, dragging the cars down the steep slopes. The fact is, this far western railroad had been built in shoddy fashion, and within 15 years had to be almost entirely refinished.

Mountain towns, mostly assembled by miners, were as raw and unfinished as those on the prairies but had the distinctive atmosphere belonging to the extraordinary heights they nestled in. One such town was Creede, Colorado, which a traveler described when his train stopped:

'At the opening of this gully . . . passengers jumped out into two feet of mud and snow. The ticket and telegraph office on one side of the track were situated in a freight car with windows and doors cut out of it, and with the familiar blue and white sign of the Western Union nailed to one end; that station was typical of the whole town in its rawness, and in the temporary and impromptu air of its inhabitants. . . . In front of you is a village of fresh pine. There is not a brick, painted front, nor an awning in the whole town. . . ; it is like a city of fresh cardboard, and the pine shanties seem to trust for support to the rocky sides of the gulch into which they have squeezed themselves. In the streets are ox-teams, mules, men, and donkeys loaded with ore, crowding each other familiarly, and sinking knee-deep in the mud. Furniture and kegs of beer, bedding and canned provisions, clothing and half-open packing-cases, and piles of raw lumber are heaped up in front of the new stores – or those still to be built – stores of canvas only, stores with canvas tops and foundations of logs, and houses with the Leadville front, where the upper boards have been left square instead of following the sloping angle of the roof.

It is more like a circus-tent, which has sprung up overnight and which may be removed on the morrow, than a town, and you cannot but feel that the people about you are a part of the show. A great shaft of rock that rises hundreds of feet above the lower town gives the little village at its base an absurdly pushing, impudent air, and the silence of the mountains around from 10 to 14,000 feet high, makes the confusion of hammers and the cries of the drivers swearing at their mules in the mud and even the random blasts from the mines futile and ridiculous.'

Mining had started out easy: you dipped your pan in likely water, carefully sifted the sand away and were left with gold. With thousands sifting the river beds, this gold soon ran out, at which point mining became big business. Huge capital investments were required to develop the deep tunnel mines, and such capital was not given to the irresponsible, half-crazy solitary wanderers of the West when it was wild. A new breed of high-stakes capital gamblers stepped in.

Of all the big strikes none surpassed the Comstock lode in Nevada, and within the palm-tingling Comstock no single find ever surpassed the Big Bonanza which four Irishmen found in 1873. Digging down 1167 feet, the silver seekers hit a solid 600 by 400 by 70 feet of silver.

The deep-tunnel mining was dirty and dangerous. Accidents were ferocious and frequent. Sometimes an entire shaft was blown to pieces along with the workers. Owners merely covered the tunnel with quicklime before sending down a new crew. Strikes began, spread and grew vicious. They were summarily put down by state and Federal militia.

Above: This interior view of a passenger coach of the type used by the Central Pacific during the 1870s shows the coal stove and type of oil lamp that were used. The seats are of more modern construction.

Right: Central Pacific engines were built here at the roundhouse in the Sacramento shops, photographed in 1891. This roundhouse survived until 1927.

When the silver and gold supplies dwindled, copper became the prime ore. This had been sneered at by the early miners obsessed with gold and silver. But by 1892 Anaconda was supplying the world with 100 million pounds of processed copper a year. Mining towns would wither and die as soon as the mines ran dry, and the restless inhabitants rushed eagerly to new strikes. Ghost towns littered the mountains and plains like cattle bones on the desert.

No matter how luxurious or interesting the journey, passengers longed to reach fabled California which awaited them with its well-publicized delights. Some travelers made a point of mixing bottles of Atlantic water with the blue Pacific once they arrived. Some stayed for extended visits, while others feasted and celebrated and then turned around to train back East.

Sacramento was the end station of the transcontinental, although the tracks continued on to San Francisco and elsewhere. Sacramento was still a garden paradise. As Mark Twain described it:

'In Sacramento it is fiery summer always, and you can gather roses, and eat strawberries and ice cream, and wear white linen clothes, and pant and perspire at eight or nine o'clock in the morning, and then take the cars, and at noon put on your furs and your skates, and go skimming over frozen Donner Lake, 7000 feet above the valley, among snowbanks 15 feet deep, and in the shadow of grand mountain peaks that lift their frosty crags 10,000 feet above the level of the sea. There is a transition for you! Where will you find another like it in the western hemisphere? And some of us have swept around snow-walled curves of the Pacific Railroad in that vicinity, 6000 feet above the sea, and looked down as the birds do, upon the deathless summer of the Sacramento Valley, with its fruitful fields, its feathery foliage, its silver streams, all slumbering in the mellow haze of its enchanted atmosphere, and all infinitely softened and spiritualized by distance – a dreamy, exquisite glimpse of fairyland, made all the more charming and striking that it was caught through a forbidden gateway of ice and snow, and savage crags and precipices.'

Robert Louis Stevenson, the amateur emigrant, had not gotten off on the plains, the prairies or the mines. He stayed on until the engines pulled into California. As they puffed over the Sierra Summit where Crocker and his crew had toiled so hard during the winter of 1866–67, he noticed a thrilling change in the ride: 'I sat up at last, and found we were grading slowly downward through a long snowshed; and suddenly we shot into an open; and before we were swallowed into the next length of wooden tunnel, I had one glimpse of a huge pine-forested ravine upon my left, a foaming river, and a sky already colored with the fires of dawn. I am usually very calm over the displays of nature; but you will scarce believe how my heart leaped at this . . . And thenceforward, down by Blue Cañon, Alta, Dutch Flat, and all the old mining camps through a sea of mountain forests, dropping thousands of feet toward the far sea-level as we went. Not I only, but all the passengers on board, threw off their sense of dirt and heat and weariness, and bawled like schoolboys, and thronged with shining eyes upon the platform and became new creatures within and without.'

A traveler had gone by railroad from the Atlantic to the Pacific. What a brave, new world!

New Patterns on the Land

'The whistle of a locomotive would be the sweetest music a resident of the broad prairies of Dakota could hear and the mere rumor that a party of railroad surveyors had been seen in a particular locality was enough to fill the hearts of every settler with joy, and cause visions of townsite and county seat speculation to color with all the beauteous hues of the rainbow his dreams at night.'

Thus the Dakota Railroad Commission described the attitude with which the people of the American West regarded the advent of the railroads in the last third of the nineteenth century. Yet the coming of the railroad to the West would transform the way of life that had drawn many of them out there in the first place. Before the railroad, the West had seemed to many and had been promoted by some

as a delicately balanced Garden of Eden. After the coming of the Iron Horse – and that very epithet for the train conveyed the sense of transformation – the West went through a cataclysmic transition. True, this new era – roughly 1870–1900 – would itself be glamorized as the Golden Age of the Wild West and assume its own mythic proportions. But now that the transcontinental railroads were in place and people of all origins and motives could make their way to and through that West, things would never again be the same. The locomotive's whistle that shattered the stillness of the vast and remote regions of the American West, the whistle that would become such a resounding echo of nostalgia for several generations of Americans – that whistle also shattered the old molds of life. The Ameri-

can West of 1900 was a far cry from that of 1870, and much of that change was due to the railroads.

Perhaps the most obvious and tangible manifestations of the effect of railroads on American life in that era were the proliferation of inventions and discoveries – the birth of technology in the development of applied science, engineering, or just plain gadgetry. The US patent office granted more patents during the last third of the nineteenth century than it had done in all the years previous. The many inventions of the period were not all directly related to the American West – let alone to the railroads. Nor was inventiveness limited to North America: both in origins and applications, inventions were all the rage throughout the advanced industrialized world of this time. But there was something about the combination of the railroads and the American West that seemed to make for a world in which inventions were sorely needed and dearly appreciated. It was as if the smoking black engines that puffed their way westward were pulling a new way of life, like a stage set being moved onto the bare continent. And this Iron Horse made everything seem possible. Optimism, opportunity, and inventiveness were part of the intoxicating atmosphere of this time and place.

Again, many of these important inventions had no direct or even apparent links with America's West – the telephone, the typewriter, the sewing machine, the vacuum cleaner, the washing machine, the electric light (and the many other

Above: This locomotive was one of the first engines of the Cascade Railroad and was built in 1862. It was photographed in 1867 at the engine terminal on the north bank of the Columbia.

Below: The last spike on the Great Southern Pacific Railroad was driven on 12 January 1883.

Left: The *Oregon Pony* was the first railroad engine used in the Pacific Northwest. It had a flatcar body cab and a rear truck.

electric apparatuses that soon followed). But these and other such inventions helped Americans overcome the distances and elements of the vast western frontier, making life more amenable and more profitable.

The telegraph, however, was one invention useful to the railroads. Invented about 1836, the telegraph was not widely utilized immediately; railroaders were a conservative lot. But in 1851, Charles Minot, then superintendent of the Erie Railroad, surprised the industry with a happy innovation. He was on a train going westward on his line when it was delayed waiting for an eastbound express. Minot already had had Ezra Cornell string telegraph lines along the Erie roadway. Now Minot saw how to use them. He telegraphed to the next station up the line, Goshen, which replied that the eastbound train had not yet arrived, indicating it was well behind schedule. Minot telegraphed to hold the train for further orders; he then commanded his own engineer to make the run regardless of the scheduled opposing train. The engineer refused: 'Do you take me for a d—n fool? I won't run that thing!' Minot then climbed into the engine cab and started the train; the engineer jumped out and ran back to the caboose. The run was made safely, of course, and at Goshen the procedure was repeated. Several stations along, the eastbound express was met at a station. 'An hour and more of time had been saved,' said Minot, 'and the question of running trains on the Erie by telegraph was once and forever settled.'

It was not settled for all railroad companies, however, and some railroads continued to experience wrecks because they insisted on maintaining rigid schedules on single tracks. But even long after the telephone came into use after 1876, the telegraph served as a necessary adjunct to running a railroad, and nowhere more so than across the long stretches of the American West.

Then there were the inventions that were of particular use to the inhabitants of the great western farm and grazing lands. There was the reaper, first demonstrated by Cyrus McCormick in 1831; it was not until the second half of the century, however, that he began to manufacture his improved reapers in a quantity to be of use to many farmers. So, too, a combine had been demonstrated in the 1830s, and soon these were being pulled by teams of horses. But it

Below: A locomotive on the portage railroad pulls away from the boat terminal on the Washington side of the Columbia River in 1867. The block-house where railroad workers sought safety from Indian attacks is on the hill in the upper left of the photograph.

was not until the 1880s, when large steam engines came into use that the farmers of the American West really made full use of the combine. Another invention that made possible the settlement of the northern plains was H L Wheeler's modification of the windmill; Wheeler's device took advantage of the prevalent winds of the region and made it possible for settlers to homestead in areas otherwise uninhabitable. Or there was the chilled-steel plow developed by John Oliver. After twelve years of work, Oliver produced a tool made of a core of good iron plus a hardened surface to which was fitted a cutting edge of tempered steel. Oliver's plow could penetrate deeper into the earth and help make homesteading possible on the hard prairie where temperatures ranged from 100° F in the summer to –40° F in the winter.

And one of the most important of all inventions for the West – although it augured an end to its 'wild frontier' phase – was barbed wire. In 1874, Joseph Glidden, an Illinois farmer, shaped the simple device (based on barbs found on natural vegetation, which he noticed that cattle avoided) that would change the face of the West. Until the advent of barbed wire, vast areas had remained essentially unsettled, open to roving herds of buffalo and their voracious competitors, the Texas longhorns, unprotected by even the most simple of fences. Barbed wire meant that the thundering herds passing to markets could be fenced off from certain land, and that railroad land could be kept from squatters and roving animals. But quite aside from the railroads' actual use of barbed wire, this was but one more

example of the inventions called into being by the settling of the American West – a settling that the railroads made both more possible and attractive.

And then there were those inventions specifically called into being by and for the railroads. By 1870, railroads were already employing some quite sophisticated technology – from battery-powered communication cords (at least in England) to Pullman sleeping cars with toilets (the first having been introduced in 1859). But in other ways, railroads remained quite primitive – and dangerous. It was George Westinghouse who developed the first air brake that would become a standard equipment on the world's railways; his first patent was in 1869, and before the introduction of the air brake, brakemen had to turn handwheels – often for as much as a half-mile before they wanted to stop. Westinghouse went on to invent a device for absorbing the shock of one car hitting another when a train stops or starts, and many other devices for improving the efficiency, comfort and safety of railroads.

In 1873 another American, Eli Janney, patented an automatic car coupler; before this invention, cars were coupled manually, and many men lost fingers or hands at this thankless task. But it should be noted that it was not until 1893, when the Congress passed the Railroad Safety Appliance Act requiring the installation of air brakes and automatic couplers on all trains, that American railroads all adopted these important devices.

Another invention for the railroads contributed to far broader changes in American life. This was the refrigerator

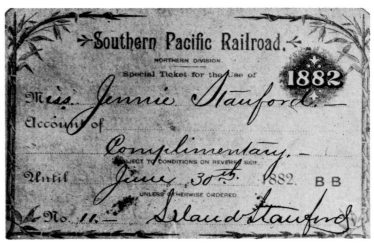

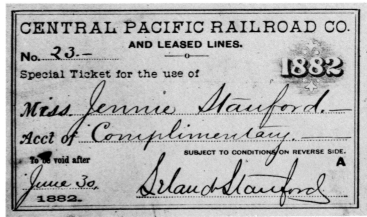

Above: The first train into Santa Barbara in Southern California on 19 August 1887 was the occasion for a big civic celebration. Most of the population of this little city was at the Southern Pacific station at the foot of State Street to greet the train when it rolled in over the line from Saugus through Fillmore, Santa Paula, Ventura and Carpinteria to the south. A special excursion train arrived later in the afternoon with visitors from San Francisco and other northern Californian cities. That night a brilliant banquet was served at the Arlington Hotel and the following day the historic event was celebrated when townspeople and visitors gathered at Burton Mound for speeches and other observances. A colorful street procession, featuring military and local bands, climaxed the occasion. The Southern Pacific Coast Line was opened from San Francisco south to San Luis Obispo in 1894 and on 31 March 1901 trains began to operate on the present Coast Line, from San Francisco to Santa Barbara, over the Santa Paula–Saugus Line and then into Los Angeles. Service on the line officially began three years later, on 20 March 1904.

Left: Southern Pacific took over the Oregon & California Railroad. On 12 November 1890 the trestle at Lake Labish, Oregon collapsed as a train full of passengers crossed over it.

Top and above: Complimentary annual passes for the Southern Pacific and Central Pacific were issued to Jennie Stanford in 1882. Central Pacific was formed in 1861, about 10 years after work began on the Southern Pacific.

car first patented by William Davis. But development of this 'magic carpet' fell to Gustavus Swift, who in 1877 began to ship dressed beef out of Chicago on a large scale. The principle of a refrigerated car was simple enough: air was blown across ice and the chilled air circulated throughout the car. Simple as it was, the perfect balance of the various elements took some years to achieve. Once it was perfected, however, many small merchants along the railroad routes who had looked forward to using such a wonderful new car were soon put out of business, as the big shippers such as Swift gained control. But refrigerator cars did open up rich new markets in perishables, aside from meat, so that both growers and consumers of fruits and vegetables were able to enjoy the benefits of this new type of railroad car. (Tank cars for liquids, by the way, had been introduced in 1865, but it would be 1910 before special tank cars for milk were introduced.)

With the introduction of electricity, still another whole dimension was added to inventions for railroads. An experimental electric locomotive had been run between Washington DC and Bladensburg as early as 1839. But it was 1894 before the first American line, a 3.6-mile stretch of the Baltimore & Ohio, was electrified, and it would be still some years before electricity came to be widely used by railroads. (The first diesel locomotive was tried in Germany in 1912, but it was 1921 before the first one was put into regular service, a Swedish-built one used in Tunisia.) But electricity was quickly applied to signaling and switching systems; an American engineer named William Robinson

patented in 1872 the electric track circuit for automatic block signaling.

The impact of the railroads on secondary technologies, such as that of the steel industry, was no small matter. The Iron Horse ate steel rails as if they were strands of grass, while the construction of hundreds of locomotives and cars also consumed large quantities of iron and steel. The steel industry grew with the railroads, which rewarded the development of improved technologies in the steel mills. Indeed, it might be said of this as of all the other inventions and technologies called into being by the railroads: if necessity is the mother of invention, then the railroads were the father during this era of American life.

But the railroads' impact extended far beyond such literal discoveries; the railroads affected every aspect of American life during the years 1870–1900. One of the major endeavors changed by the presence of the track that was winding its way throughout the populated West was the cattle industry. Ranching had been good business for some time, but after 1867 it was to become one of the most lucrative of all. At that time, it was found that the Texas longhorn could be crossed with Hereford stock, with a plump, strong breed resulting. Soon it would be found that cattle could survive the colder northern winters, fattening on the green gold of the prairies.

The buffalo, of course, already grazed on the sweet, shoulder-high grasses of the American prairies. Bunch grass, buffalo grass, bluejoint turkeyfoot, bluestem, and sand dropseed, among other nutritious plants, grew in abundance. But the railroads would soon play a crucial role in disposing of the peaceful and indigenous herbivore: within 20 years the buffalo had practically disappeared and overgrazing had made desert of the rich grazing lands. In the mid-1880s the cattle business would itself collide with another new industry – sheepherding – causing dreadful repercussions to both businesses before an equitable arrangement was worked out between them.

As the railheads pushed west, a young man, brought up in the cattle business, took note. It was Joseph McCoy who first saw the potential rewards for the cattle business in having a railhead in mid-Kansas. His interest would change the face of middle America.

Joseph McCoy had grown up in a large family whose father was in the beef trade. In 1867, when Joseph saw the railroad creeping across the plains, he bought most of the town of Abilene, Kansas, a 450-acre lot which included a few cabins and a saloon. Its importance to him was that it strategically straddled the proposed route of the railroad tracks projected to reach Abilene some four months after the deal was made. McCoy proceeded to buy the best lumber from Missouri and put up stockpens strong enough to contain 3000 head of livestock at a time. He also built a

machine which could weigh 20 cows at once. He did not worry about too much else, although an 80-room hotel sprouted up soon enough for rich traders. First of all McCoy invested $5000 in advertising to attract the cattlemen. He offered $40 an animal, delivered in good condition to Abilene. McCoy would then entrain the cattle to the lucrative eastern markets. St Louis, Missouri, the current shipping depot, would be by-passed by his dusty dream in Kansas.

A flamboyant mesmerizer, McCoy figured that if the cowboys would take his bait, he would be able to deliver 200,000 head of cattle in 10 years. His advertising caught the imaginations of the ranchers and he saw the first herd arrive only four months after his advertising campaign began. That would be just about as long as it took the herd to maneuver the Chisholm Trail up from Texas. The first season, 1000 carloads had been loaded at Abilene, and in New York it was soon reported that McCoy could load a train of 40 cars in two hours. Nor did he fake his weights as some shoddy entrepreneurs were wont to do. It was a notorious practice to heavily salt the cattle's food, then lead them to water just before weigh-in, creating watered-stock. (The term was later transposed to the practice of

Above: TNO locomotive *Stowe* of the Southern Pacific's Texas lines on the turntable at the El Paso roundhouse, laden with fuel. The first train arrived in El Paso in 1881.

Inset left: Locomotive *Ann* of the Cascade Railroad was built by the Vulcan Iron Works at Scio, Oregon in 1862 and worked for the Oregon and California. It was reported that the engine saw later use by the Southern Pacific during branch-line construction in Oregon.

Below: At the Salem, Oregon station in 1892 a hotel stagecoach and horse-drawn carriages collect and drop off passengers. At the rear of the station a regular full-size train accepts passengers and small horse-drawn local cars of the Salem Street Railroad Company await more customers.

issuing more paper stock than a railroad company was worth, a dishonest financial transaction which brought many a railroad to ruin.) But McCoy was an honest man, and in four years he sent over two million fat, healthy animals to the East. He became the King of Cattle.

One of the crucial components of this new West was the cattle drive. The first, and perhaps the most romantic of all cattle trails was the famous Chisholm Trail that led from South Texas to Joseph McCoy's Abilene. This most famous of all cattle trails was traced out by Jesse Chisholm, a half-breed, half-Scot and half-Cherokee. The trail was begun in 1867 when Chisholm mapped the flattest route between south Central Kansas and his own place on the Canadian

Below: Southern Pacific Locomotive No 2006, a 4-6-0, was formerly Central Pacific Locomotive 208 built by Cooke in 1876. It was renumbered CP 1573 in 1891 and SP 2006 in 1901. The engine was scrapped in 1935.

River in Texas. It then continued onto the ranches of South Texas. Sometimes as many as 28 herds would stomp the trail in a day, each herd numbering somewhere between 1000 and 3000 head of cattle. Usually the ratio of cowboys to cattle on these long trips was one for every 250 animals. The cowboys had their horses, of course, with extras in case of rustlers and other disasters. The herd would be led by a pair of longhorns which instinctively took the lead in the arduous trek. Some bovine leaders were used over and over again.

The trail from the Texas Panhandle to booming Kansas railheads took roughly four months of danger. Crossing the Red River and Indian territory, struggling against harsh weather conditions and pervasive dust, remaining alert for the sneak attack of rustler or Indian, took stamina and courage. Sometimes at the Red River, waiting for waters to recede from some storm in the headwaters, as many as 60,000 animals might be milling anxiously on the shore. Merely to keep the animals separate in their own herds would cause trouble and delays. The plaintive lullabies of cowboys on the watch could be heard all along the Chisholm Trail at night. Cowboys were not singing for their women, but to calm the skittish longhorns who were apt to stampede at the drop of a frying pan.

The marriage of the railroad with the open grassland marked the heyday of the American cowboy. During the rip-roaring years between 1867 and 1887, when the beef cattle industry became big business, the cowboy emerged as the unlikely knight of the prairie. On the arduous drives to the raucous railroad towns of booming Kansas, the cowboy usually received a lowly 25 dollars a month. It took two months' pay just to buy a pair of cowboy boots. He also cared for ranches sometimes larger than most eastern states, fattening indestructible Texas longhorns on the green gold of the prairies, all the while living a life of roughness and isolation. The cowboy became a most engaging folk hero. His legend spawned whole industries of exhibitions and rodeos, of books, magazines, photographs, firearms, fashions and songs.

Once he got to his railhead towns, the cowboy made up for his arduous tasks by having wild fun in the legendary Wild West cowtowns. Abilene was one of the most typical in its raucous ways. Abilene boasted saloons, brothels and gambling joints, some stores and not much else. For sleeping and eating, cowboys had to retire to their chuckwagons. At any one time, these might encircle the town by the hundreds, their campfires burning merrily, songs and laughter cheerfully mixing with the groans of heady hangovers and depressions caused by bad luck at the gambling halls.

Abilene attracted the most unsavory elements of society to prey upon the transient cowpokes ready for a spree after the long trek on the Chisholm trail. Marshals were appointed to control the volatile situation, but seldom had much effect. One of the most famous marshals of that first cowtown of the West was 'Wild Bill' Hickock who had been a 'bad man' himself, having chalked up an estimated forty killings before he threw in with the law. This dandy of the prairie shot only two people while marshal, one of them a friend of his, a policeman. Hickock was a snappy dresser, a former Union Army scout and a gambler. He preferred to keep a firm hand on his town from the round table in the gambling den.

When the wild way of life became too much for newly arriving settlers, the towns were divided in two. On one side of the tracks the hell-raisers could set up shop. On the other side, the more solemn and respectable members of the community could reside undisturbed. Hickock held his office for eight months in 1871 at $150 a month, but killing the policeman discouraged the good people of Abilene. They decided they had had enough of 'Wild Bill' and enough of cattle, too. They put an ad in the newspaper requesting that cattlemen no longer use Abilene as their destination point for shipping to eastern markets. Once the cattle were no longer being shipped from Abilene, the town took the stern road of homesteading and respectability. (Twenty years later the Eisenhower family would settle here, and a future President would grow up in the by-then back-water town.)

Starting about 1872, then, the Texas cattle drovers began to head for other towns, such as Wichita and Ellsworth, further west in Kansas. As other railroad tracks began to snake across the West, other colorful and equally rowdy towns flourished: Dodge City along the Santa Fe route, Oglalla and Cheyenne along the Union Pacific tracks. The opening of the Chisholm Trail had marked the beginnings of the new era of the Wild West. But 20 years later the railroads had spread north and south from the transcontinental, new inventions and technologies were changing the patterns of food production and transportation, and the Chisholm Trail no longer seemed so important. The railroads that had created the demand for these cowboys thus contributed to bringing about their end. But unlike so much else in the West that disappeared when the railroads let off their full steam, the cowboys did not simply vanish into thin air. Righteously rowdy, bowlegged and lovelorn, independent and eminently able, they walked out of the austere landscape of prairie and plain into the imagination of the world.

If the railroads helped to change the nature of America's cattle business during these years, they also had a major impact on the companion activity of farming. For a long time Americans had imagined a nation in the pattern of New England stretching across the continent. Small self-supporting farms employing people's energies to keep them clothed, fed, and – most important of all for a true republic – independent. Even as late as 1860, land was still the measure of Americans' independence: six million people worked in agriculture, only four million worked in non-farm enterprises. These non-farm enterprises were for the most part local, the owner and his employees working and living within a short distance of each other, familiar with and respectful of each other's lives.

After the Civil War, farming attracted millions to try their luck. Both native-born Americans and the new immigrants began to move westward. Acreage under cultivation would rise from 407,212,000 in 1860 to 878,798,000 in 1910. The number of farms would rise from 2,033,000 in 1860 to 6,361,000 by 1910. Production also rose dramatically, enabling the American farmer to feed the newly teeming cities. Production of wheat went from 173 million bushels in 1860 to 635 million bushels in 1910; corn went up from 838 million bushels to 2,886,000,000; cotton from 3,841,000,000 bales to 11,609,000,000. This very success glutted domestic markets and forced Americans to sell in the world's markets. America was on its way to becoming the breadbasket of the world.

But not all was perfect in this new American paradise. Farmers faced many problems: soil exhaustion, drought, frost and floods; over-expansion and over-production left them vulnerable to changing demands; high mortgage rates and interest on the new heavy equipment put a constant demand on their cash flow. Meanwhile, the farmers had become hostage to the railroads – at least in the western states. The population centers had often shifted with the railroads; many of the new farmers and other settlers had been actively recruited by the railroads, which had all that land to 'give away' – but with strings attached. Railroad freight rates began to rise, fairly or otherwise, and the farmers had to ship their produce or lose everything. Soon a farmer had to begin to think like a businessman, and soon, too, farmers had to turn to their banks for capital and short-term loans to tide them over. Many a once-proud, able-bodied family returned from the American West bitter and broke, to take their place in the newly emerging social order of factory employment.

Responding to the new pressures on lands in the West, the US Congress passed three acts between 1873 and 1878 that were intended to help the new settlers. The Timber Culture Act granted an additional quarter of a section (160 acres) to any homesteader who agreed to plant trees on a quarter of the land. By virtue of this legislation, 65,292

Locomotive No 73 of the Big Four's Southern Pacific line is about to come off the turntable at the Monterey roundhouse in 1887.

homesteaders received 10 million acres of land during the 15 years it remained in effect. Undoubtedly many individual families profited from this act, but ultimately the big lumber companies would profit the most.

The second act passed by Congress was the Coal Lands Act, which offered public coal-bearing lands to anyone who could pay $10 to $20 an acre. Not more than 160 acres were permitted per person, and 320 acres was the limit to any group. But like most such acts passed by Congress to limit the purchase of public land, this was easily circumvented, and rich coal-bearing land was eventually transferred to profiteers – sometimes for as little as a glass of beer.

Finally, in 1878, Congress enacted the Desert Land Act, designed to encourage development of arid western lands in need of irrigation to become useful. Homesteaders had found that quarter sections (160 acres) were often unprofitable in the Great Plains and Southwest. Congress granted any person paying 25 cents an acre an entire section, or 640 acres, if that individual irrigated some part of the claim within three years; if this were done within that period, then the entire section could be purchased for only one dollar more per acre. It was later estimated that 95 percent of the claims made under this act were fraudulent and ended up in the hands of big cattle ranchers. To prove irrigation, an owner – in the presence of the appropriately corrupt official – might merely dump a pail of water on the dry earth.

Given the high hopes that attended the passage of such laws, plus the euphoria with which the country greeted the meeting of the engines at Promontory Point in 1869, it is hard to imagine how quickly the dream of the Golden West turned into a nightmare for many people. How could this have happened? For one thing, the land-grant system that

had been so instrumental in getting the railroads started in the West attracted some rather dubious characters. Some of these men would become legends if not heroes in later years, if only because they made so much money that history has felt compelled to take notice of them. But they also wrecked the hopes and plans of millions of other Americans.

Cornelius Vanderbilt, for instance, was not really a builder of railroads, nor was he interested in developing the West. But by judicious manipulation of railroad stocks he would amass a fortune estimated at $100 million. Vanderbilt owned the New York Central outright and had all but destroyed the great Erie Railroad with the help of the shady Jay Gould and the shoddy Jim Fisk, both of whom became rich from the venture (stealing some $6 million in one fraudulent deal alone). Gould went on to build railroads in the West, but his Santa Fe line had to be essentially rebuilt within 15 years because of Gould's milking every last penny of profit for himself. These men were not real builders like James J Hill, who constructed the Great Northern Railroad with his own money and without the aid of land grants. Rather, they were unscrupulous entrepreneurs and there were no laws at that time to prevent their destructive shenanigans.

Even the Big Four of California – Crocker, Huntington, Hopkins, and Stanford – to whose credit the heroic building of the Central Pacific is due, even they spent the rest of their days gouging their fellow Westerners, creaming off profits that hardworking people risked everything to build up. When Collis Huntington or Mark Hopkins poured over their books and found that a town was prospering, for

instance, up went the railroad rates at once; if a town was doing badly, down went the rates until a turn in fortunes occurred.

To be sure, there were also some highly respected men who were involved in managing railroad securities, but even they sometimes got in over their heads. One such was Jay Cooke, whose banking company agreed to underwrite the Northern Pacific Railroad in the early 1870s when it began to penetrate into the rich northwest. Blinded by his own high hopes, Cooke went some $40 million into debt, having agreed to support a 7.3 percent dividend on all first mortgage bonds. Cooke was not in control of the details of the building of the road which was paying out over $50,000 per mile on rail everyone knew could be built somewhere well under $20,000. The price of bonds fell. Buyers from the East Coast and from Europe rushed to pick up the cheap but guaranteed paper. Cooke could not meet his obligations and closed his bank doors on 18 September 1873. Other railroads were pulled down in the ensuing panic. Millions of honest investors who had generously supported their local rail company with their savings, confidently expecting a fair shake, were swept into the shambles as banks tumbled after railroads, crashing to the ground.

Thirty-seven banks and brokerage houses closed the same day as Cooke. Two days later the New York Stock Exchange was shut for an unprecedented 10 days. Other banks were forced to close down, affecting the fortunes of thousands of merchants and farmers. Some 5000 businesses failed in the first year, and 10,478 went bankrupt before the country turned a corner in 1879.

The Panic of 1873 was essentially the result of years of over-trading, over-production, over-speculation, over-issues of paper money and inflated prices. It was also a 'coming home to roost' of all the early indebtedness caused by over-building and over-capitalization of early railroad endeavors. The economy had been running on high for 12 years, and a letdown was inevitable. The failure of Cooke was merely the snowball that started the avalanche; it was not in itself responsible for the conditions that led to the disaster.

The Panic of 1873 spread its misery across the land, so that for two years those out of work in America outnumbered those with jobs. As desperate men moved around the nation looking for vanishing opportunities to work, they cast a shadow on the American dream – and not so incidentally, generated a new lingo that was also involved with that of the railroads. The basic name for men who worked on the railroads was 'stiffs,' and there were numerous variations on this, such as 'bindle stiffs,' those who carried their own bedding. There were also the itinerant or seasonal laborers on the railroads who were known as 'gandy

Above: Engineer James D Taylor stands with the engine pilot of Union Pacific 553 at the station in Columbus, Nebraska around 1882.

dancers': their name came from the gandy, the tamping bar they used, which in turn took its name from the Chicago manufacturer of the tool. Now these regular railroad workers were joined by the 'hoboes,' again a name that had been around for some time, although its exact origin is unknown; originally 'hobo' did not refer to tramps or beggars but to migratory workers, unskilled or jacks-of-all-trades perhaps, but definitely seeking seasonal or casual jobs. The lingo of the hoboes had its own distinctions: 'cronickers' were those who had their own cooking pans; 'dynamiters' those who sponged their mulligan stews; and there were those who were low down in the hobo hierarchy – pokey stiffs, white line stiffs, ding bats, fuzzy tails, jungle buzzards, straight crips. But there were also those known by the accidents they had suffered while trying to 'nail a drag' (that is, catch a ride on an already moving train): accident to the eyes, the 'blinkies'; to arms, the 'wingies'; to arms and legs, the 'righties' and 'lefties.'

The swelling of the numbers of these colorful types confirmed that all was not well in the Golden West. Yet

during this time of massive unemployment of the 1870s depression, railroads continued to pay from eight to ten percent dividends on all stock. Even that was acceptable, since most Americans believed in their hopeful hearts that they might be lucky and strike it rich themselves. Thus it was not until the railroads began to cut wages that resentment also began to express itself. The first cut came early in 1873, and one of the first major strikes called by a union in America followed shortly, that of the railway workers in Chicago that year. Even then it took some time before the massive effects of the depression also allowed many Americans to see that railroad owners were not suffering.

In 1877, however, the Pennsylvania, the Erie, the New York Central, and the Baltimore and Ohio railroads joined in putting another 10 percent wage cut into effect – while still paying close to 10 percent dividends. The pent-up fury of the railroadmen burst like an exploded steam boiler on the nation. (Perhaps it had not helped, either, for workers earning a maximum $3 for a 12-hour day to learn that young William Vanderbilt had this year inherited the $100 million his father had acquired, much of it from his railroad investments.) One of the first violent strikes in America occurred that July, when protesting Baltimore & Ohio employees walked off their jobs; before they returned, Federal troops had been called in, over 60 people had been killed, and many more wounded. The strike was joined by

82

Cars loaded down with great redwood logs from northernmost California head south, where the lumber was to be used to build the city of San Francisco.

EXCELSIOR
REDWOOD CO.
EUREKA, CAL.

DIA. 11 FT. 9 IN.
LENGTH 18 FT.

Top: Locomotive No 166 was built by the Central Pacific Railroad Company at the Sacramento shops in 1886 or 1887. This is one of A J Steven's Valve Motions engines, commonly called CP Monkey Motions or CP Monkeys because the return rod, or 'galloping rod' as the engineer called it, looked like a monkey hopping along when the engine was in motion.

Above: Locomotive *San Mateo* was photographed in 1866 hauling a passenger train over the old San Francisco & San Jose Line. This was the first line out of San Francisco, and completion of the road was celebrated with a formal opening on 16 January 1864. The San Francisco & San Jose became part of the Southern Pacific in 1870.

Right: Two crew members line up the tracks of the turntable to turn locomotive No 417 of the Santa Fe railway at the roundhouse in Richmond, California. The movable circular tables were developed in the early eighteenth century to allow cars to change directions easily or to transfer them to other tracks.

the railroad workers in Pittsburgh, where again the Federal troops were called in, over 20 were killed, and a terrible fire (set to drive the troops away) ended up destroying some $10 million worth of property, including 2000 freight cars. It took almost 10,000 Federal troops to break that strike in Pittsburgh, but the fact is that the men returned to work within a week, and without any betterment of their working conditions or without preventing the cut in their wages.

What had happened to turn the immense goodwill felt by the American public – and particularly the appreciation of those in the West – into distrust if not outright hatred for the railroads? Inept leadership, willful mismanagement and downright dishonesty all contributed to the change. Unregulated, careless, even unscrupulous use of the vast powers and resources in rail companies also changed the public's attitudes. Perhaps an even more crucial factor was the ambiguity of the place of the railroads in American society that nagged at the nation. Were they semi-public utilities or simply money-making machines? Small villages, middle-sized towns, bustling cities, even whole states, had put themselves deeply in debt to help bring railroads to their regions. For what purpose, they now asked themselves. Railroads seemed to be destroying their very way of life, tipping many people who had never been poor into the trough of poverty.

For railroads at this time had the power to make or break whomever they pleased – certainly small farmers and small businessmen could not stand up to them. Stockholders, meanwhile, felt no responsibility toward the railroad employees or their customers. And the depression that followed Cooke's railroad venture began to end only about 1879, leaving things worse for the people of the American West. Owned by absent money-men who had no regard for local interest, trains now by-passed towns and villages that had gone into debt to help build their own local railroad companies. In the time-honored way of big business, the big companies had eaten up the smaller ones, and the new bodies were being run to produce dividends rather than to fulfill local business needs. Railroad officials were hired from far away, beholden to some distant superiors who neither knew nor cared about local situations.

Most particularly, the rebate system was ruining many small businessmen during this era. The practice was simply to charge less for larger or longer freight hauls – to offer a rebate, that is, to the big customers. The result was that it might cost less to ship coast-to-coast than to a town half-way across the nation. This system, enhanced by big business's bribery of railroad officials and the railroads' bribery of State and local government officials, handicapped the small businessman. Big businessmen such as Rockefeller, Carnegie, or Swift took advantage of the rebate practice to ruin their competitors, adding them like scalps to their own gargantuan belts. Meanwhile, less lucrative rail routes were likely to remain monopolies, charging exorbitant rates that subsidized runs to cities where the owner wanted to compete with other railroad companies for trade. And the final blow came when the big railroads collaborated, openly and otherwise, to pool their resources for their own benefit.

When this period began in the 1870s there was little or no legal protection against such unfair practices and it seemed that most Americans – especially those scattered throughout the vast lands of the West – were powerless to fight or change them. Yet by the time the century was turning, there were some signs of resistance, some outright struggles, and some changes. These came from several directions. But it might be said that it was the farmers who were first roused to protest the wasteful, wanton destruction of the American way of life. And if any individual deserves credit for rousing these farmers, it was Oliver Hudson Kelley, an obscure young clerk in the government's Department of Agriculture. Kelley had been born in 1826 into a well-to-do family in Boston. His eager enchantment with life had early on taken him West where he worked first as a telegraph operator, then as newspaperman. Settling in Minnesota, he began compiling reports for the Agriculture Department. He noted the desperate straits that farmers were in, not so much in his adopted state, as in other areas such as the South and further west. Observing the situation with intense concern, Kelley decided that it was the farmer's fatalistic attitude that was obstructing what should otherwise be successful and fulfilling lives. In 1867 with six other young idealists, he resigned his job to found an educational and social gathering, which he called the Patrons of Husbandry. He began it as a secret society on the lines of the Masonic Order of which he was a member, with the usual rituals and trappings. But the group soon gave up this side of its meetings and sought to focus on immediate problems of importance to farmers. The members quite predictably

came to be called Grangers because of their custom of meeting in 'granges' (originally a farmhouse, but here applied to the hall as a sort of manor).

At first it attracted few members, but when it undertook to challenge the Goliaths of railroads, suspicion dissipated and six years after its inception, the Grange Movement had magnetized 858,000 members into its ranks. Their single greatest accomplishment was enactment of the so-called Granger Laws to curb, through regulation, the worst of railroad abuses.

The first of these was passed by the Illinois legislature in 1874. Among its other provisions was one which demanded that freight rates be based strictly on distance traveled. Although ultimately unworkable, this was intended to meet one of the greatest railroad abuses of the time. Iowa and Wisconsin followed Illinois with their own statutes. These two States set up the first railroad commissions and attempted to fix maximum rates for freight haulage and passenger service. Farmers and small businessmen were making their voices heard in legislatures that had been deaf to their voiced concerns for years. Not many months had passed before 42 States and Territories had enacted similar legislation to curb the railroads.

The main points that farmers and their allies demanded were equal rates for long or short hauls. And no rebates to special customers for large hauls. Limitation on dividends

Below: The *Shou-wa-no*, a Mogul 2-6-0 type, was placed in service in 1871 and was the first freight locomotive on the Denver & Rio Grande Western Railroad.

Opposite top: Railroad construction progresses up the line near Whitefish, Montana around 1903. The forward part of the gang lays the ties and spaces them for the crew behind. Protected by tarpaulin from the hot sun, they lay the steel rails under the supervision of the foreman.

Laying Steel

was another demand. These, it was said, should be based purely on traffic returns. A great many railroads were despoiled because money which should have gone into good construction in the first instance, and secondly into upkeep and repair, was, instead, funneled into the pockets of the stock manipulators. A five percent dividend on traffic profits was considered fair.

Fairness would have to be legislated, the Grangers said, so that workers got a fair return for their work and were not bargaining chips in someone else's game. Railroads should also be required to deal fairly with all other railroads – neither blocking lines nor favoring special customers. Railroads should also be required to publish their rates and stick to them. In an attempt to preserve some of the smaller independent lines that were disappearing into the maws of the giants, the Grangers also asked that consolidations be forbidden. At the very outset of the development of railroads, George Stephenson had predicted, 'where consolidation is possible, competition is impossible.' Now he was being proved right. Cut-throat competition, whereby one road set out to crush or gobble up all others, was not deemed the same as competition that allowed most of the other participants to continue in the running.

State legislatures were the first government bodies to respond to the rising anger of the nation against railroad practices. Neither the Presidency nor the Congress was especially responsive in the early years to demands for helping the public fight the railroads – in part because they were influenced by their personal and financial relations with those who owned such big businesses as the railroads, but also because they simply had not yet perceived their role as requiring them to advance the public's welfare. But eventually, Congress and the Presidency would act. In 1887 they passed the Interstate Commerce Act, setting up a five-man commission to see that railroad rates were just and 'reasonable'; to forbid double-tiered rates for long and short hauls on freight carriers; and to stop discriminatory rates between competitive and non-competitive localities. And in 1890, Congress and the Presidency adopted the Anti-Trust Law (often associated with the name of the Senator from Ohio who introduced it into the Senate, John Sherman); this made illegal 'every contract, combination in the form of trust or otherwise, or conspiracy, in restraint of trade or commerce among the several states, or with foreign nations.' (Ironically, one of its early applications would be against a railroad workers' union – in the Pullman Strike of 1894.) Such laws would not in themselves assure the end to abuses by the railroads, but they would put the American people on record as being ready to restrain them.

As the Grangers began to succeed in changing the laws of the land to favor individuals and smaller enterprises, the railroads naturally began to fight back by fair means or foul. They had at first been caught unawares by the angry backlash against their willful practices; they had counted on a docile, cowed public. So railroads began to take their case to the courts – all the way to the Supreme Court. The Supreme Court was in some ways the last American governmental institution to come around to supporting social change – bogged down as the court was in precedent that had little relevance to the new conditions of the industrial age. On 1 March 1877, however, ruling on *Peik vs Chicago*, the Court declared for Granger interest, finding that a

state has the power to regulate intrastate and interstate traffic originating within its boundaries. The same day, in a related case, *Munn vs Illinois*, the Supreme Court found that a state has power to legislate warehouse and intrastate rates. Although the Supreme Court would later be induced to reverse itself and strike down these state-authorized regulations, the tide was turning.

And an important lesson was being learned in these years between 1870 and 1900, a lesson for which the railroads were partly responsible. Americans were learning that they would have to gather together, to define their needs and goals, to figure out their step-by-step tactics, if they were to right the inequities that had befallen many of them, particularly small farmers and workers. And what the Grangers were doing for the farmers, unions were beginning to accomplish for workers of all kinds. It was no coincidence, either, that among the first and most enduring of efforts by American laborers to organize themselves were the Railroad Brotherhoods. The first of the so-called 'Big Four' was the Locomotive Engineers Union, founded back in 1863. The Railroad Conductors Brotherhood was organized in 1868; the Brotherhood of Locomotive Firemen and Enginemen was founded in 1873; and the Brotherhood of Railway Trainmen was founded in 1883. (Eventually the last three would join together, but the Locomotive Engineers have always remained independent.) Because railroad jobs were often dangerous to life and limb, these railroad workers tended to be more interested in accident and life insurance and retirement benefits – compared, that is, to other unions' emphasis on wages and hours – but in that respect, as in others, the Railroad Brotherhoods proved to be in the vanguard of the American labor movement.

Not that it was all upward and onward for the railroad workers. In 1894, for instance, there occurred one of the most notorious labor-management-government confrontations in the nation's history, the Pullman Strike. Since the late 1860s, George Pullman had dominated the manufacture of sleeping, dining and other specialized railway cars, and in 1881 he had founded a residential town, next to Chicago, where many of his employees lived, paying rent to the Pullman Company. Because of a decline in business in general, Pullman announced in 1894 that he would be cutting wages of all its employees – many of them worked on the special cars themselves – but he would not lower the rents in the company town.

As it happened, only the year before the American Railway Union had been organized, based in Chicago and headed by Eugene v Debs. In 1870 Debs had gone to work at the age of 15 as a locomotive fireman. He quit that job in 1875, but by 1880 he was the secretary-treasurer of the national Brotherhood of Locomotive Firemen as well as editor of its paper. Wanting to get away from the crafts unions, Debs helped to found the first attempt at an industry-wide union in America, the American Railway Union. This union, led by Debs, petitioned the Pullman Company for a restoration of pay; this was not only refused but the union representatives working for Pullman were fired. A strike was called, first in Chicago, but soon it spread throughout the USA as employees of various railroads refused to handle the Pullman cars.

Below: The first Pullman sleeping car was put into service in the United States in 1859. Vestibules, such as in this Southern Pacific sleeping car, were first built into passenger cars in 1887.

As railroad traffic in the nation slowed down, especially that connecting with Chicago, the Pullman company appealed to the US Attorney General Richard Olney. With President Cleveland's support, Olney got a federal court injunction on the grounds that the movement of the US mails was being interfered with. When resistance continued, President Cleveland ordered federal troops to Chicago to maintain the mail service. To enforce this injunction, the Federal government, ironically, invoked the Sherman Anti-Trust Act of 1890, which declared illegal all 'combinations in restraint of interstate or foreign commerce.'

Within a week, the strike was broken. But there were numerous gains and losses from this strike, not all of which could have been foreseen. President Cleveland, for one, lost the support of many working people. Another who came under attack was Robert Todd Lincoln, the oldest son of Abraham and Mary Lincoln; he had become the counsel for the Pullman Company, and his role in breaking the strike was contrasted to his father's emancipation of the slaves. Eugene Debs was held in contempt of court for defying the injunction and served six months in jail; during that time, however, he read about socialism and in 1897 he changed what was left of the American Railway Union into what became the Socialist Party of America, whose candidate for the Presidency Debs would be in five elections.

But the impact of the Pullman Strike went beyond individuals. In the immediate term, it set a pattern of legal procedures that would prevail in America for many years to come: namely, if it could be charged that unions were acting in restraint of trade or in endangering the national welfare, courts could enjoin the unions from further strike activity and/or federal troops could be called out to maintain services. But in a broader sense, the railroad workers in the Pullman strike – just as the Grangers in their struggles – had accomplished something else. They had brought to life the sense of social purpose above and beyond mere self-assertiveness and self-gain. In reaction to the excesses of the big railroads and big businesses such as the Pullman Company, Americans bestirred themselves to grander goals and nobler dreams. The underlying sense of fairness characteristic of Americans would exert itself and a demand for social justice would enter public debate in a meaningful manner.

And no matter how individual settlers and workers fared during these years, American farming and industry and

Above: Freight loads of lumber are brought down from the lumber yards inland to west-coast ports and are piled at the dockside to be loaded on ships.

Above left: Locomotive No 1212, originally No 124 and called *Umpqua*, is one of the old iron horses of the Central Pacific. It was built by the Globe Locomotive Works at South Boston in 1868, but was broken up for scrap at the beginning of the twentieth century. Russel P Clark, draftsman from the Sacramento Drafting room, took this photograph while the train was in service at Folsom Prison near Sacramento. Two convicts escaped on this engine by getting in the water tank and hiding until the train left the prison. Following that incident a padlock was put on the well hole. Johnny Cash later wrote the song called 'Folsom Prison Blues' about hearing train whistles from inside this prison's walls.

Above right: Locomotive No 28 approaches the water tower at a break in the line. The first centralized traffic control on the Southern Pacific was installed in 1930 between Sacramento and Stockton to ease the load of heavy traffic on the rails. Signaling tells the driver which route to take and at what speed he should travel, ensuring safety on the rails.

Overleaf: A Whitney Timber Company locomotive at work on the feeder line to Southern Pacific's Tillamook Branch in Oregon. The rod engine was the *Big Jack* and the climax geared engine was the *Molly O*. The California & Oregon Railroad, incorporated in 1865, later became part of Southern Pacific.

society in general prospered. The West was populated, cities grew, farms fed the people. America in 1900 *was* different from that of 1870. And this age of the Golden West had been a time of paradox, of great successes and dismal disappointments, of opportunities gained and squandered, of inventiveness and repression – changes so drastic as to have no social precedent in which to operate. But some lessons were learned. And it can be fairly claimed that the railroads that were so crucial to opening up the West also played a crucial role – willingly or otherwise – in opening up some of these new directions in American society.

There are several images that emerge as the century is about to turn. One is of the 'Great Crush Crash' of 1896, organized between Waco and Hillsboro, Texas by a curious American, William George Crush. Two engines are hurtled full throttle at each other to crash head on while 40,000 spectators watch bemused. Rather surprisingly, only three bystanders are killed and not many injured. Or there was another train crash, in Vaughan, Mississippi, on 30 April 1900, when Casey Jones was bringing his *Cannonball Express* into the station only to see that the tracks are blocked. Instead of jumping out, Jones holds onto the brake and thus minimizes the impact so that no passengers are killed – only he himself is crushed to death. A black railroad worker, Wallace Saunders, will write a ballad about this event that eventually becomes the basis for various folk songs that will go on to make Casey Jones a legendary hero in the United States and in many other parts of the world.

But it would be false to see the century turning on railroad crashes. The western frontier itself might be regarded as coming to a close by now; in fact, it is sometimes said to have been 'officially closed' in 1890 when the federal government terminated the land-grant programs for both the railroads and private settlers. And although the 'gasoline carriage' had been invented and was beginning to come across the horizon, it would be many years before automobiles seriously challenged the railroads for transportation of large numbers of people or volume of freight. No, in 1900, railroad trains were 'kings of the road,' not only in American West but throughout the world. Passenger and freight traffic were increasing as were the size and speed of the trains themselves. The 'golden age' of America's western railroads lay ahead.

The Golden Age

By the turn of the century, five great lines – the Southern Pacific; Atchison, Topeka and Santa Fe; Union Pacific; Northern Pacific; and Great Northern – stretched across the United States from the Mississippi River to the Pacific Ocean. Two more, the Western Pacific and an extension of the Chicago, Milwaukee, St Paul and Pacific to Seattle, were added in the first decade of the twentieth century. The Western Pacific was completed from San Francisco to Ogden, Utah in 1909.

Some 70,000 miles of track had been laid in the western United States by 1890. However, there was no true coast-to-coast line owned by one company. The only real North American transcontinental rail lines were in Canada. The existence of two coast-to-coast rail lines in Canada before the end of the nineteenth century was nothing less than remarkable, considering that western railroad building had started much later in Canada than in the United States, and that Canadian railroad builders faced far more formidable physical obstacles than did their counterparts below the border.

The first Canadian railway was built in 1836 to provide a portage system between the St Lawrence River at Montreal and Lake Champlain. This line was incorporated into the Grand Trunk Railway, which opened in 1856 between Toronto and Montreal. The fact that Canadian lines tend to be called 'railways' rather than 'railroads,' as they are in the United States, is indicative of the British influence. The building of the Canadian rail system started as a British colonial undertaking, and the term 'railway' had been used in Britain from the earliest days. In the United States, the term railroad was generally adopted, perhaps as a further assertion of independence from Britain.

British railway builders soon found that conditions in Canada were very much different from those in Britain. So while the term railway persisted, Canadian railways, including locomotives, rolling stock, tracks, bridges and trestles, were, of necessity, much like those in the United States.

The incentives for building railways in Canada were as much political as economic. Like the United States, Canada had vast stretches of land that had to be opened to settlers. The remote provinces needed rapid and dependable communication with the more thickly settled eastern regions if they were to become truly a part of a united Dominion. The pressing need for railways in areas where such an expensive undertaking would not likely be im-

mediately profitable soon led to direct government participation. Eventually, a unique network of publicly and privately owned lines, operating successfully side-by-side, evolved in Canada.

The Canadian Pacific, the major privately-owned rail system in Canada, came into existence as a transcontinental railway. The building of this railway was an incredible accomplishment, a feat that had been dismissed as impossible when it was first proposed. An Imperial Commission sent a survey team to find a route in 1857. After spending four years in the western Canadian wilderness, the surveyors submitted a negative report which included the

Above: On 30 June 1886 the first Canadian through-train completed its journey from the Pacific to the Atlantic at Port Arthur, Ontario. The Canadian Pacific Railway, originally a privately owned company, built the first direct route between the east and west and was completed within 10 years. The 2879-mile journey from Montreal to Vancouver took six days in 1886, twice the time it takes today. James J Hill, one of the owners of the company, left it to form the Great Northern company in the United States.

Below: Great Northern 2-10-2 *Santa Fe*, No 2100, was the first of 30 Q class engines built in 1923 and designed for hauling heavy freight. The straightforward design, typical of heavy freight cars at that time, featured a conical boiler with Belgaire firebox and a Vanderbilt tender with a 15,000-gallon water- and 25-ton coal-carrying capacity.

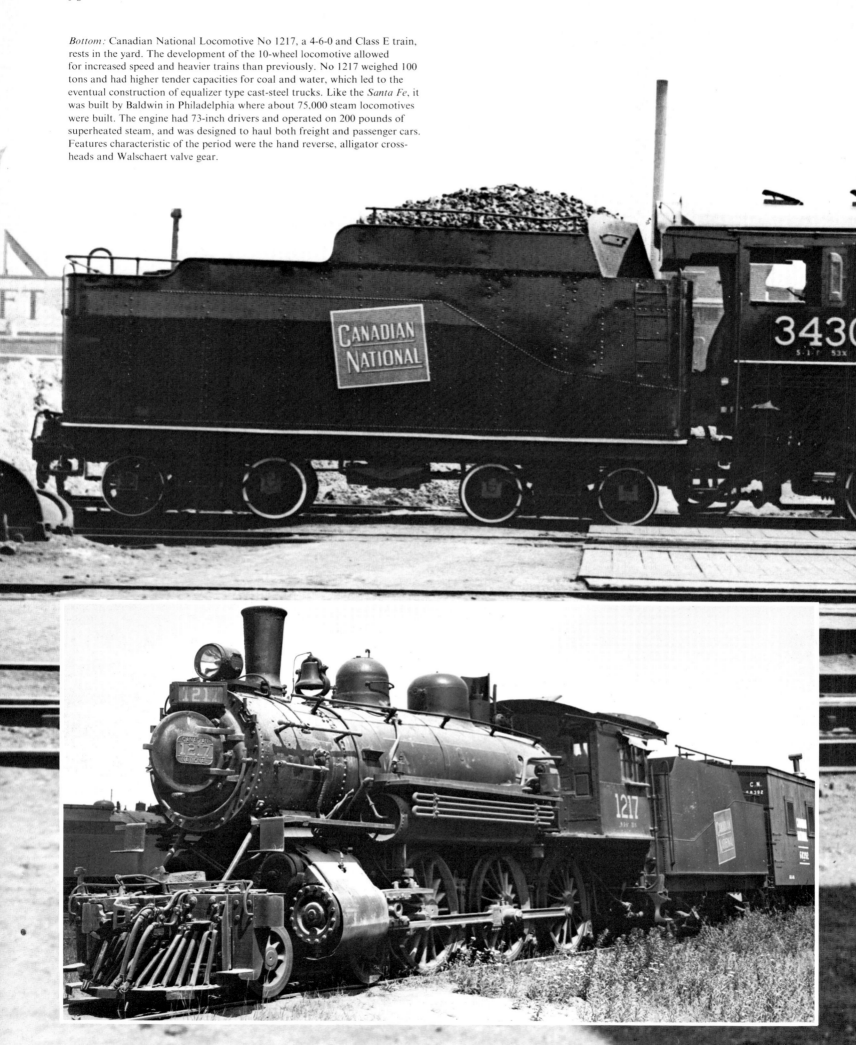

Bottom: Canadian National Locomotive No 1217, a 4-6-0 and Class E train, rests in the yard. The development of the 10-wheel locomotive allowed for increased speed and heavier trains than previously. No 1217 weighed 100 tons and had higher tender capacities for coal and water, which led to the eventual construction of equalizer type cast-steel trucks. Like the *Santa Fe*, it was built by Baldwin in Philadelphia where about 75,000 steam locomotives were built. The engine had 73-inch drivers and operated on 200 pounds of superheated steam, and was designed to haul both freight and passenger cars. Features characteristic of the period were the hand reverse, alligator cross-heads and Walschaert valve gear.

Below: This sleek Canadian National No 3430 2-8-2 is similar to the *Santa Fe*, a Baldwin-built locomotive Class Q 2-10-2 of the Great Northern. It also resembled the *Mikado* Class O which was one of the heaviest locomotives built and designed with 280-pound steam pressure that was later reduced by 30 pounds.

Railroads of Western Canada

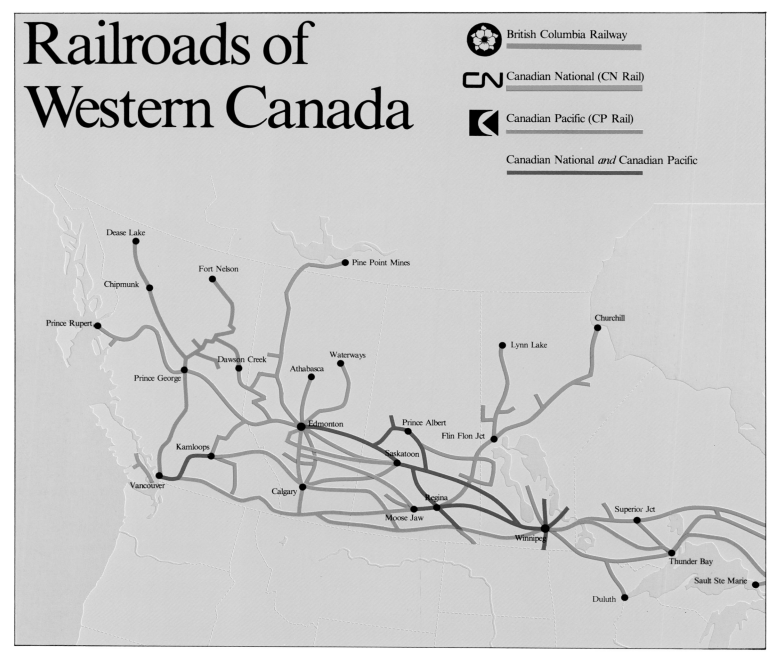

British Columbia Railway

Canadian National (CN Rail)

Canadian Pacific (CP Rail)

Canadian National *and* Canadian Pacific

statement: 'The knowledge of the country as a whole would never lead me to advocate a line of communication across the continent to the Pacific.' The apparently impregnable mountain ranges – the Canadian Rockies and the Selkirks – were the barriers that convinced the surveyors to issue the negative report. However, they did note the discovery of Kicking Horse Pass in the Rockies, the place where the line would eventually be built through the mountains. Eight years later, a surveying expedition sent out by the Surveyor General of British Columbia delivered a more favorable report in which they claimed to have found a possible route. However, the Canadian Government was not moved to action until British Columbia threatened not to join the Dominion as long as they were cut off from the rest of Canada. So in 1871, British Columbia agreed to be admitted as a province in the Dominion of Canada only when the Government of the Dominion agreed to start building a railway through the mountains toward British Columbia within two years.

However, four years were to go by before construction was actually started on 1 June 1875, six years after the Union Pacific was completed at Promontory, Utah. Two com-

panies were formed to build the line. Eventually, these merged to form the Canadian Pacific. The company received a subsidy of $25 million, 25 million acres of land, and two previously completed eastern railroads.

The Rockies were by no means the only obstacles faced by the railroad builders. Spruce swamps, called muskegs, had to be crossed, drained or bypassed. Massive rocky outcrops had to be blasted in conditions that included minus-forty-degree temperatures in the winter, and clouds of biting flies and mosquitoes in the summer. One of the most difficult stretches was the northern shore of Lake Superior. The terrain was precipitous, and the lake waters along the shore where the line ran were unpredictable. Many observers suggested that attempting to build a railway through this wilderness was foolhardy, proposing instead that the area be by-passed by ferrying railroad cars across the lake to railheads in the United States and reconnecting with the Canadian Pacific in Manitoba. The leading promoter of this scheme was one James J Hill, who proposed that his railroad, the St Paul, Minneapolis, and Manitoba, provide the link. Ironically, an American, William Cornelius Van Horne, general manager of the Canadian Pacific, pushed

Above: A powerful Canadian National 4-8-4 locomotive, No 6157, at the station in the days before steam power was phased out. Southern Pacific built a class of 4-8-4 locomotives in 1930 whose main frames and cross-stretchers were built as a single casting. A booster engine underneath the firebox increased the tractive effort of the engine nearly 20 percent.

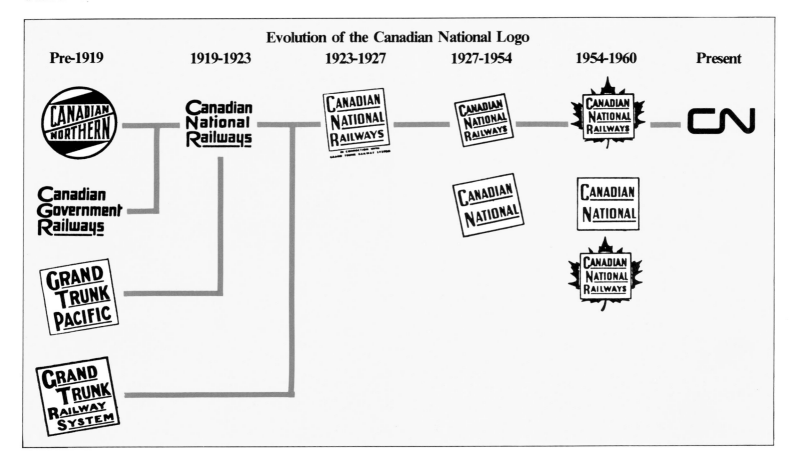

Evolution of the Canadian National Logo

| Pre-1919 | 1919-1923 | 1923-1927 | 1927-1954 | 1954-1960 | Present |

the original plan for the project through, and made the Canadian Pacific an all-Canadian railway.

Despite the monumental efforts involved in draining swamps, lowering lakes and diverting rivers, sections of track disappeared into the swamps over and over again. Spikes had to be heated to keep them from cracking when driven into the ties, which themselves often splintered into shards in the temperatures of 40 and 50 degrees below zero.

The impact of these natural obstacles was compounded by one financial crisis after another. The government was not inclined to give the developers any more money, and by the mid-1880s the venture was near bankruptcy. The line was unwittingly saved by Louis Riel, the French-Indian renegade who had led the unsuccessful Northwest Rebellion in 1870. In 1885 he had raised another army of rebels, and the situation in the Northwest Territories was grave. Van Horne put the uncompleted railway at the disposal of the Canadian military. Troops were moved into action in a record time of four days, and the rebellion was put down. This incident convinced the government that a transcontinental railway was important to national security, and more money was appropriated to finish the railway, albeit reluctantly.

Canadian National Railways formally came into existence in 1923, when all the government-owned lines in Canada were merged. The term, however, had been in general usage since 1918–19, when the government started to take over transcontinental lines built after the completion of the Canadian Pacific. These lines, such as the Canadian Northern Railway (CNR), prospered as carriers of immigrants into the Canadian interior. The Grand Trunk became transcontinental with the building of the Grand Trunk Pacific line in 1915. When the tide of immigrants dried up during World War I, the railways were in trouble. After the war, renewed need for transportation and the fear of a Canadian Pacific (CP) monopoly encouraged the formation of CNR.

By the time the CNR absorbed the Grand Trunk in 1916, this oldest of Canadian railroads had expanded into a large network in eastern Canada and had lines extending across the border into New England, Michigan and Indiana. Other components of the CNR, including the Intercontinental Railway and the Transcontinental Railway that ran from Quebec to Winnipeg, were government-owned from the start.

The CNR today has more than 25,000 miles of track, including the world's longest steel cantilever railway bridge, stretching 1810 feet over the St Lawrence River at Quebec.

The CP and CNR have been in direct competition. Each line offered its own luxurious transcontinental service. The CP's most famous service was the Transcontinental Canadian, and the competing CNR train was called the Super Continental. These trains, which offered spectacular scenery in addition to impeccable service, were typically overbooked in the summer. The Super Continental has been discontinued, while the Transcontinental Canadian is run by Via Rail, a Corporation set up in 1978 to run CNR and CP passenger trains.

The American western frontier did not end at the Pacific Coast. In 1867, Alaska was bought from Russia, and the United States had obtained what was to become its wilderness frontier. The first attempts to build a railroad in Alaska did not start until 1903, with the privately financed Alaska Railroad planned to run from the port of Seward

A 1930s photograph of the Saskatoon freight yard in Saskatchewan, full of Canadian Northern box cars, including a few refrigerator cars. Specialization in rolling stock increased after 1925, especially in refrigerator cars for transporting perishables. Later box cars were built much bigger than the ones shown here, up to 85 feet long and 18 feet high.

Below: This lineup of dazzling Canadian National Railway engines at Railway Week in June 1964 at Belleville, Ontario shows the range and development of engines from the steam age to the present. Four old steam engines, Nos 247, 40, 5700 and 6167 and diesels No 6400 and 6534 complete the range.

Bottom: A closeup of No 6400. Long-haul transcontinental railroads were beginning to move toward diesel-powered locomotives by the mid-1930s in the quest for more speed.

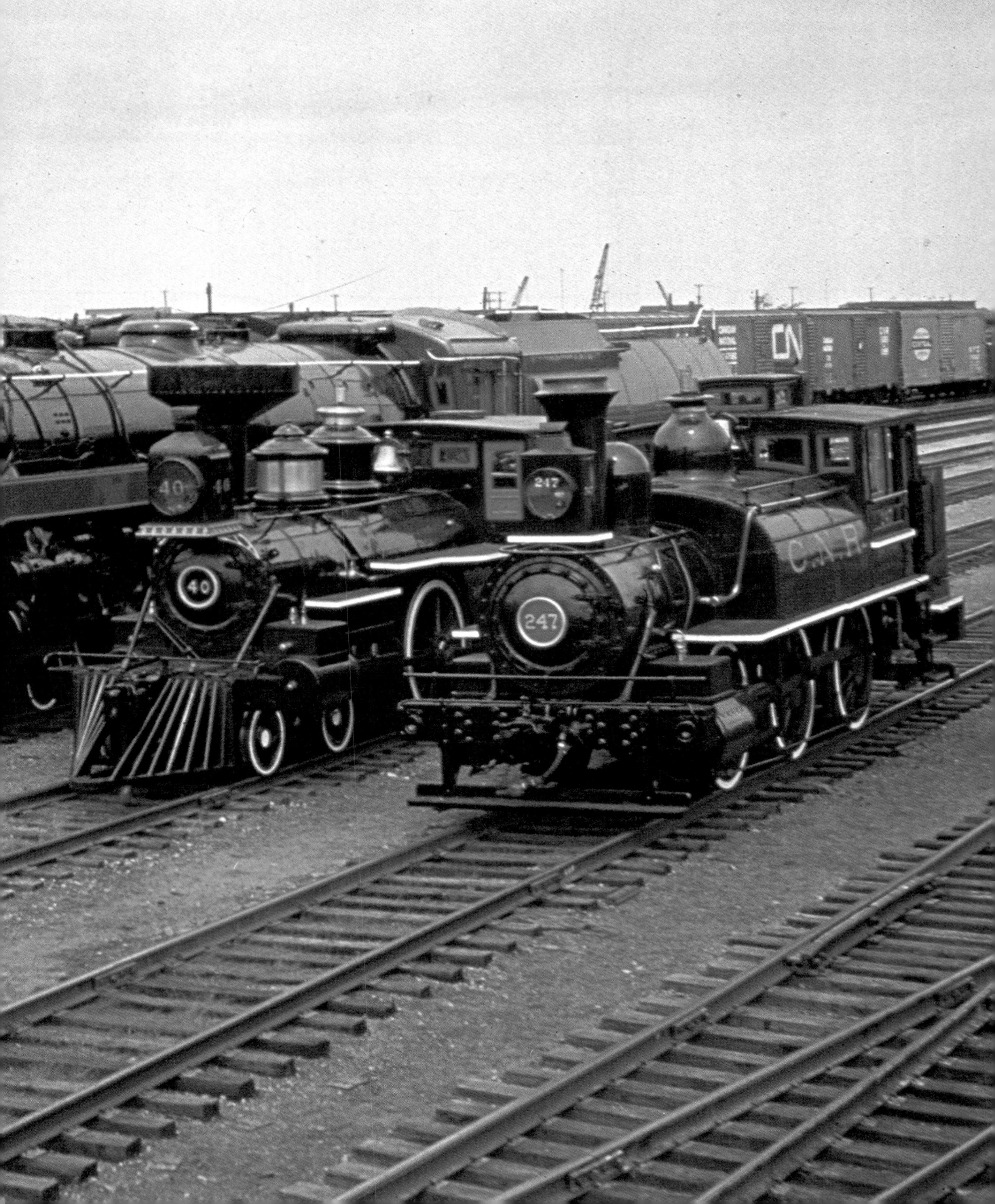
40
40
247
247
C.N.R.
CN

104

This photograph was taken in the 1920s at the San Francisco yard, showing the stunning contrast between two relics from the old days of steam. The *C P Huntington*, built in 1863, was the third locomotive built by Central Pacific and was later renamed SP No 1. It now belongs to the State of California and rests in the railroad museum in Sacramento. The much larger No 3631, a 2-10-2, was of early twentieth-century vintage.

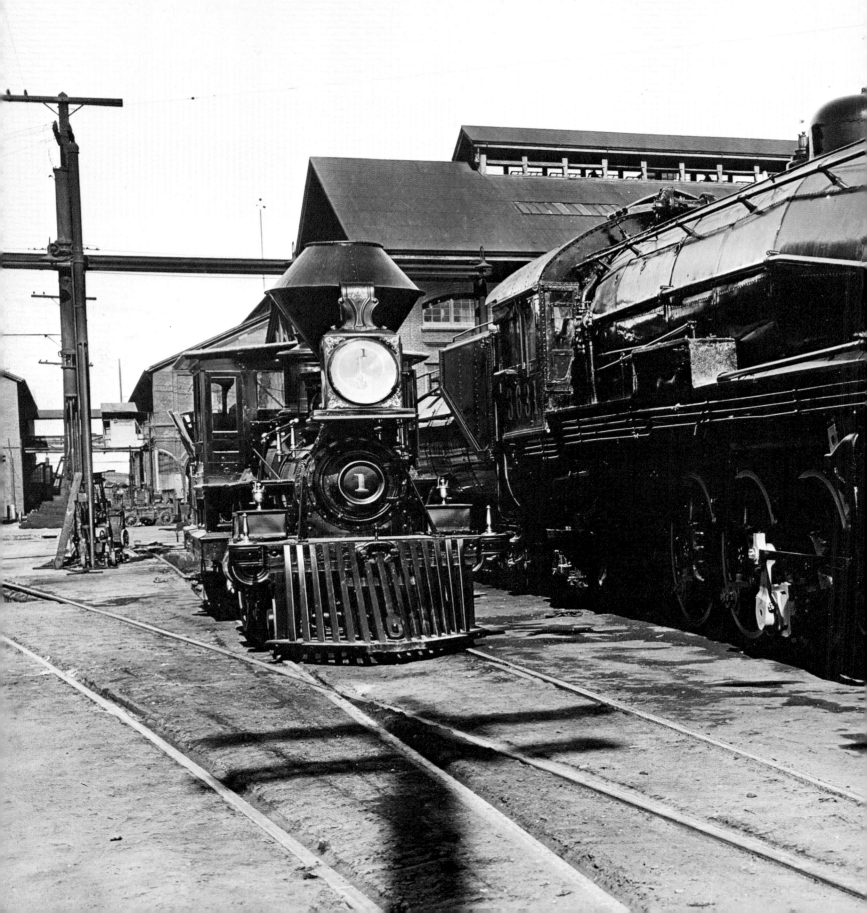

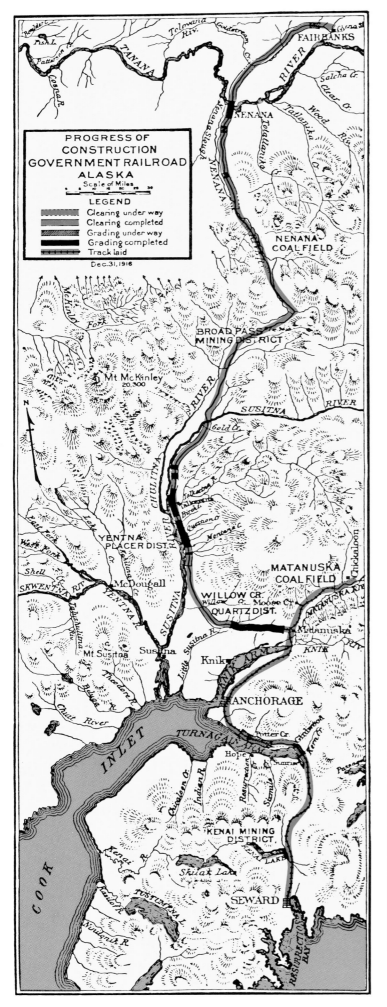

to the gold fields at Fairbanks. As might be expected, the venture was a financial disaster. By 1910, only about a sixth had been completed. The Federal Government took over the project in 1914, and it was completed in 1923. Carrying both freight and passengers, the Alaska Railroad continues to operate at a profit in an area where air travel is the dominant form of transportation.

The White Pass and Yukon Railway (WP&Y) was another railway built to meet the needs of the Alaska gold rush. Opened in 1890, the narrow-gauge (3 feet) line runs from Skagway in Alaska to Whitehorse in Canada's Northwest Territories. In the early days at Whitehorse, passengers could continue on the company's river steamers up the Yukon River to Dawson. Still in business in the 1980s, the company specializes in containerization. It acquired the world's first container ship in 1953, a move that overcame the problems of incompatibility of gauge with other railroads.

The WP&Y runs a vintage passenger service complete with wooden coaches and a 60-minute sourdough lunch stop as a tourist attraction. Since the trains are mixed freight and passenger, a passenger can load his or her car on the train. It is one of few remaining working narrow-gauge railways in North America.

The first half of the twentieth century is widely regarded as the 'golden age' of American railroading. Safety, speed, and comfort had improved greatly since the days of the robber barons. Railroads were slowly regaining the favor of public trust which they had previously destroyed through exploitation. Once more, the public regarded the railroads as the very symbol of efficiency and high standards of performance. People set their watches by the comings and goings of trains. In many quarters, 'railroad time' was synonymous with correct time.

As providers of cheap and efficient movement of goods and people, the railroads had helped to make the United States a leading world industrial power, and its people enjoyed one of the highest standards of living in the world. Although it was not apparent in the 1900s and 1910s, the very prosperity the railroads helped to create would contribute to their decline. Henry Ford made his first Model T in 1908. Apparently there were quite a few Americans who had the means to equip themselves with a Tin Lizzie. By 1928, some 15 million had been produced and sold. A new generation of Americans was beginning to discover and enjoy the new mobility. They could go where they wanted to go when they wanted to go there, unfettered

Above: An Alaska Railroad switch engine, photographed in 1983, operates in the southeastern part of the state.

THE ALASKA RAILROAD

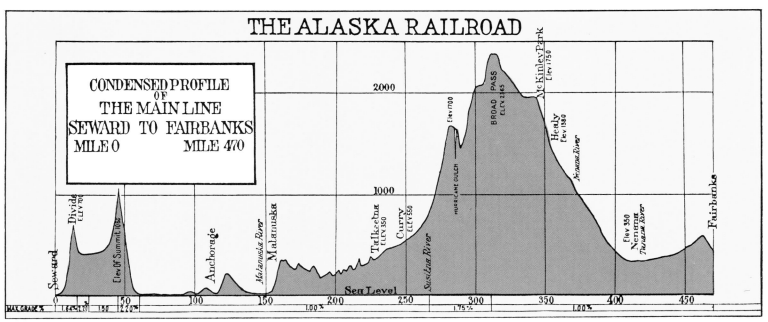

CONDENSED PROFILE
OF
THE MAIN LINE
SEWARD TO FAIRBANKS
MILE 0   MILE 470

The Alaska Railroad

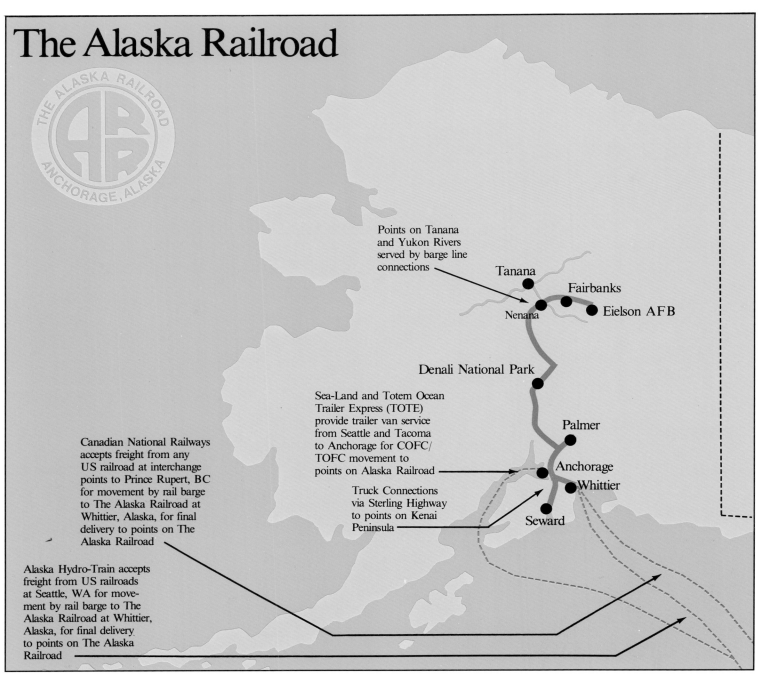

Points on Tanana and Yukon Rivers served by barge line connections

Tanana

Fairbanks

Nenana

Eielson AFB

Denali National Park

Sea-Land and Totem Ocean Trailer Express (TOTE) provide trailer van service from Seattle and Tacoma to Anchorage for COFC/ TOFC movement to points on Alaska Railroad

Palmer

Anchorage

Whittier

Truck Connections via Sterling Highway to points on Kenai Peninsula

Seward

Canadian National Railways accepts freight from any US railroad at interchange points to Prince Rupert, BC for movement by rail barge to The Alaska Railroad at Whittier, Alaska, for final delivery to points on The Alaska Railroad

Alaska Hydro-Train accepts freight from US railroads at Seattle, WA for movement by rail barge to The Alaska Railroad at Whittier, Alaska, for final delivery to points on The Alaska Railroad

Left: A steam crane was called into action after an accident involving passenger cars on the Great Northern Railway main line at Badrock Canyon, between Belton and Whitefish, Montana. The canyon was named for the rock that hung over the old coach road on the other side of the river.

Below: Steam crane No 2030 was manufactured by Industrial Works of Bay City, Michigan in 1909 for Southern Pacific. Capacity without outriggers was 16 tons at a 20-foot radius and 22 tons at a 16-foot radius. Without outriggers the capacity was 60 tons at a 20-foot radius and 120 tons at a 17-foot radius.

by the demands of a railroad timetable. And at the same time, there were few, if any, observers who had the temerity to suggest that the curiosity known as the flying machine would ever be a threat to the mighty railroads.

The railroads soon helped to make the adjective 'wild' an inappropriate description of the West. A home in Butte could have the same amenities and luxuries as one in Boston. The railroads brought pianos, clocks and fine china to the Wild West, where they were likely to be affordable to more people because the same railroads brought products of the West such as beef and grain to eager buyers in the East.

The railroad was an important part of life in the relatively remote towns of the western plains and mountains. Arrivals and departures were the high point of the day, and in many towns much of the population dropped whatever they were doing to go to the depot whenever a train came in. In many towns, the tracks ran through the town, often right through the center. Tracks came to have sociological significance in many towns and cities, as they provided convenient dividing lines between the 'good' and 'bad' parts of town. 'The wrong side of the tracks' still implies social and economic disadvantage. In speaking of the train culture, one can hardly leave out its leading lady: steam. More than anything else, the word 'steam' evokes the vision of railroading's Golden Age. All the romance and legend, the majesty and grandeur of railroading are captured in that word.

Steam locomotives had been in general use on American railroads for some 40 years when the golden spike was driven at Promontory, Utah. But western railroads presented a problem that called for locomotives far more powerful than those used on eastern railroads in the 1860s and 1870s. That problem was getting over and through the Rocky Mountain passes. This need led to the development

of locomotives that were some of the most awesomely powerful machines ever made for land travel. There are those who think the sight of an articulated 2-8-8-8-2 (28 wheels!) locomotive huffing mightily up a mountain pass, filling the sky with massive clouds of black smoke and white steam, represents the most glorious image of the Golden Age.

The logical first step in increasing the power of locomotives was increasing the number of driving wheels. This principle was apparent quite early, and 4-4-0 engines were built in the United States as early as the 1830s. Locomotives with the 4-4-0 wheel arrangement, with four connected driving wheels on each side (four-coupled), became the standard of railroads throughout the world. With the opening of lines across the Rockies, it was soon painfully apparent that the standard 4-4-0 workhorses would not do the job in the Rocky Mountains. Before the end of the nineteenth century, a ten-coupled, fourteen-wheel locomotive, the *El Gobernador*, had been built for mountain use. Designed by A J Stevens for the Central Pacific, the behemoth proved to be too rigid and heavy for the tracks in use at the time.

In the last quarter of the nineteenth century and into the twentieth century, the common practice in western railroads was to use double, triple, and even quadruple-heading on mountain runs, using two or more locomotives coupled together to pull a train. This technique was fairly expensive, since a crew was needed in each locomotive. From the practice of multiple heading came the idea of compounding, combining two or more locomotives in one flexible (articulated) hinged unit, equipped with a boiler big enough to supply all. One crew could do a job that previously required several.

Many of the compound locomotives used on American mountain lines were designed by a man named Anatole Mallet. In a typical Mallet locomotive, the rear engine was fixed, and the leading one could pivot as well as move sideways. This arrangement made it possible for the big engine

to negotiate the winding curves on the mountain lines. The first of these locomotives used in the United States was a 0-6-6-0 built in 1904. The Great Northern started to use 2-6-6-2 types in 1906, and 2-8-8-2 locomotives were used on the Southern Pacific starting in 1909.

For passenger and mixed traffic, the Union Pacific used a 4-6-6-4 called the *Challenger*, and the Northern Pacific employed 4-8-4 *Northerns*. Introduced in 1927, some 1000 *Northerns* were built. The *Challenger* was first made in 1936 and about 200 of these were assembled.

For hauling freight over the mountains more power was needed. From 1926 on, the Union Pacific used a huge 4-12-2 aptly named the *Union Pacific*. For sheer numbers, the record is probably held by the Atchison, Topeka and Santa Fe's *Santa Fe*. Introduced in 1915, some 2200 of these 2-10-2 locomotives were built. Ask a locomotive aficionado what was the greatest steam locomotive ever built, and the answer you are likely to get is Union Pacific's 4-8-8-4 *Big Boy*, introduced in 1941. Although only 25 were built, these huge machines are widely considered to have been the ultimate locomotive, the high point of all the power and glory of the steam era. Weighing more than 1,100,000 pounds, a *Big Boy* hauling 4000 tons up a mountain pass would consume about 22 tons of coal and 12,000 gallons of water in an hour.

Below: In January 1911 this rotary engine was called out to clear the tracks of the Great Northern Railway after snow slides in the Rocky Mountains near Fielding, Montana. These machines could clear drifts of up to 20 feet deep, which was the diameter of its blades.

Opposite top: A long freight train is hauled across the mountains by Great Northern steam locomotive No 2032. This Mallet-articulated 2-6-6-2 Class L engine was built by Baldwin in 1906–07. The 144-ton engines of this class had $20/31 \times 30$-inch cylinders and used 200 pounds of saturated steam. In addition they had slide valves and Walschaert valve gear.

Opposite bottom: Santa Fe No 1793 (2-8-8-2) and No 3782 (4-8-4) steam through Raton Pass below Wooten, Colorado.

Left: The *Overland Limited* of the Southern Pacific approaches 16th Street Station at Oakland. The photograph was probably taken around 8 May 1908, when Admiral 'Bob' Evans brought the American battleship fleet to San Francisco. The battleship *Iowa* is in the background.

Below: Southern Pacific's Martinez-Benicia Bridge across Suisan Bay, 35 miles from San Francisco, was the largest and heaviest railroad bridge west of the Mississippi River. The double-track structure was 5603 feet long and was opened for traffic on 15 October 1930. The entire project, including about six miles of track approaches, was constructed in the remarkably fast time of 18 months at a cost of almost $10 million.

Below: Great Northern's *Empire Builder*, one of the great name trains of all time, is seen here at the St Paul Union Depot on the day of its inaugural, 11 June 1929. The $5 million fleet of eight luxury trains cut five hours from previous schedules between Chicago and Seattle, making the run in 62 hours and 45 minutes. Great Northern introduced the country's first postwar fleet of streamliners in 1947, continuing the *Empire Builder* tradition. A completely new fleet of streamlined cars went into service in 1951 and dome cars were added in 1955.

Other steam engine developments of the twentieth century included oil-burning locomotives, turbines and streamlining. A number of railroads made use of oil-burners, including the Atchison, Topeka and Santa Fe, and the Southern Pacific. Quite a few railroad executives considered oil burners more efficient and economical to run than coal burners, but that assessment depended on the comparative prices of coal and oil. In the 1930s and 1940s, when these engines started to come into greater use, the price of oil was quite often less than that of coal. Oil burners eliminated the need for a fireman to shovel coal, but there were also coalburners that had automatic stokers. However, neither of these mechanisms enabled most railroads to eliminate the expense of a fireman. Union regulations

on many lines stipulated that a fireman be in the locomotive no matter what kind it was – coal, oil, diesel or electric. This and similar practices were called 'featherbedding,' and helped contribute to the decline of the railroads.

Oil burning made it possible to build 'cab-in front' locomotives that improved visibility for the engineer. These were used on the Southern Pacific, so much so that these 2-8-8-4 locomotives became somewhat of a Southern Pacific trademark. The added visibility was particularly welcome in the many tunnels on the SP's mountain routes.

The twentieth century also saw the development of turbines that provided direct circular motion to the wheels of the locomotive. The Union Pacific tried a steam turbine that turned a dynamo to provide electricity for motive power. The Chesapeake and Ohio and the Pennsylvania Railroad built experimental turbines in the 1940s. The last steam locomotive built for the Norfolk and Western was a turbine. Named the *Jawn Henry* after the 'steel-drivin' man' of song, it was not considered a success. The theoretical

Southern Pacific No 3312 crosses the river at Santa Rosa, New Mexico, hauling a Santa Fe coal car and Pacific Fruit Express reefers – ventilated refrigerated cars for carrying foodstuffs. Pacific Fruit Express Company, incorporated in 1906, is jointly owned by Southern Pacific and Union Pacific.

advantage of the turbine was that by producing circular motion it eliminated the intermediate back-and-forth reciprocal phase of pistons moving in cylinders. This was supposed to be more efficient than pistons, but in practice it did not work out. These engines required more hours of maintenance than did piston engines.

Another innovation intended to improve efficiency, streamlining was nothing more than placing a curved cowl over the engine or curving the horizontal aspect of the boiler. The streamlining was intended to reduce air resistance. There was nothing wrong with the concept, although there were complaints that streamlining tended to reduce accessibility to some parts, making servicing more difficult.

Neither oil-burning, turbines, nor streamlining were able to hold off the conversion to diesel which took place rapidly after World War II, discussed in the following chapter.

Some of the narrow-gauge lines operating in the United States stayed in business well into the twentieth century.

Most of those in the West were in rugged mountain country, and many earned their livings hauling logs. Western narrow-gauge railways were almost all three-foot gauge.

Although the locomotives used on these lines were of necessity smaller than those run on standard gauge, they had to be very powerful if they were to pull their loads up mountain grades. Steam locomotives used on these lines had a distinctive look. To improve stability, the frames were placed outside the wheels and the connecting rods drove on outside, separate cranks.

Logging railroads were characterized by 60-degree curves, grades of eight percent, sloppily-laid track, and trestles that required courage, foolishness or both to cross. These conditions called for locomotives that were able to drive on all wheels with high traction and had flexibility on all axles. The best-known and most peculiar-looking of these was the *Shay*, also called the side-winder. The boiler was offset to make room for a vertical steam engine that drove all the wheels through external shafts, universal

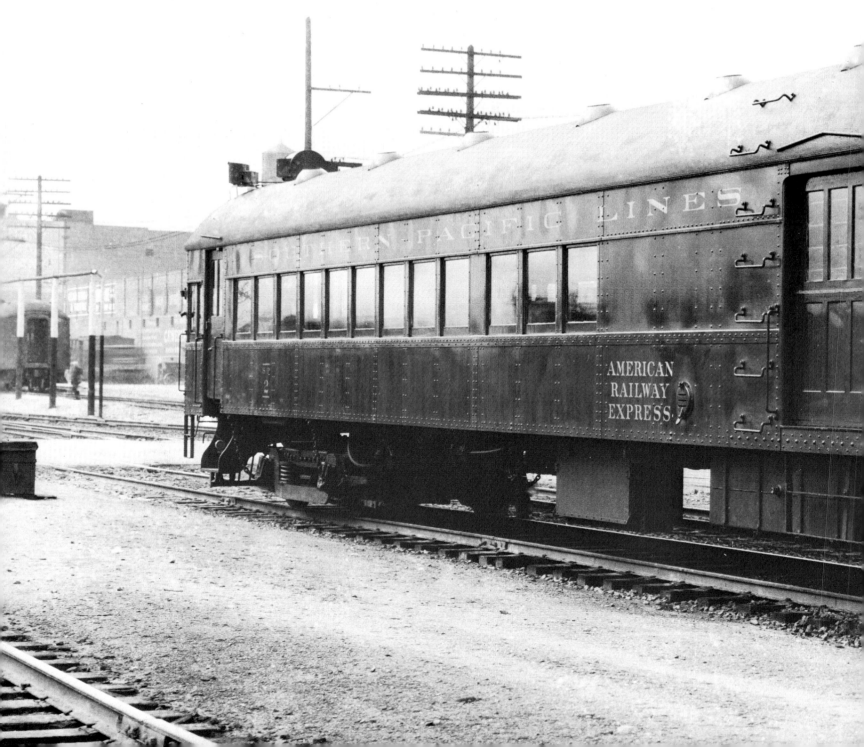

Left: The strange McKeen gasoline-powered passenger car, looking more like a submarine than a train, at the La Jolla Station in Southern California, around 1919.

Below: This Southern Pacific baggage car for American Railway Express was powered by a combination of gas and electricity.

Above: The train at the Banff station in Alberta, Canada prepares to depart after dropping off visitors to the area.

Below: The *Daylight*, southbound from San Francisco to Los Angeles, rounds Horseshoe Curve north of San Luis Obispo, California in the late 1920s. This train was inaugurated in 1922 as the *Daylight Limited*, and in 1927 it became the *Daylight*. The train was streamlined in 1937 and in 1940 was renamed the *Morning Daylight*. The name was again changed in 1952 to the *Coast Daylight*, which it remains today. It was dieselized in 1955.

joints and bevel gears. A few can still be seen on museum lines. The *Hiesler* vied with the *Shay* for strangeness of appearance. Its V-2 engine cradled the boiler. The *Climax* locomotives, also used on logging lines, looked much like the engine used today on the Mt Washington Cog Railway in New Hampshire.

Most narrow-gauge railroads were small, local lines, but some major lines, notably the Denver and Rio Grande, were built in narrow gauge. The general idea was that narrow gauge was cheaper to build, particularly in mountains. However, the money saved in construction was often lost in the costs of off- and on-loading where the narrow gauge met the standard.

The Denver and Rio Grande was forced gradually to convert to standard gauge. Its last narrow-gauge run, the 250 miles from Alamosa to Farmington via Durango, was not only the last commercial narrow-gauge operation in the United States, but was also the last steam locomotive-hauled freight common carrier operation. This service continued until 1967.

A steam passenger operation still runs on the Denver and Rio Grande. Recently sold, this is a 'pleasure' or tourist line that runs a spectacular 45 miles up the Lost Souls Canyon and back. Called the 'Silverton Train,' it operates only during the summer tourist season, and boasts the highest earnings per passenger mile of any passenger train in the United States. A section of narrow-gauge track formerly owned by the Denver and Rio Grande is now run by the State of Colorado. Called the Cumbres and Toltec Railroad, it is also a summer-season tourist attraction.

The early years of the twentieth century was also a period of progress in general passenger comfort. By the 1920s, dangerous wooden cars, heated by wood-burning stoves, had been largely replaced by cars of metal construction, heated by hot water or steam systems. Suspensions were improved, and six-wheel – rather than four-wheel – trucks became the general rule for passenger cars. The improvements in comfort were particularly welcome on the long western runs.

Despite the labor difficulties experienced at the end of the nineteenth century, the grand tradition of elegance and comfort was still evident in the Pullman cars of the twentieth century. George Pullman, a man whose name has become synonymous with railroad luxury, had started to work on sleeping cars in the 1850s. In 1859 he built a sleeping car converted from a day coach. The first sleeping car constructed by Pullman from the wheels up was ready for passengers in 1864. The typical arrangement of the Pullman sleeping car was evident by this time. Upper berths folded up against the upper walls during the day and were pulled down to become beds at night. The day seats were converted into more comfortable lower berths. Pullman rented rather than sold his luxurious cars – consisting of dining, parlor and private cars as well as sleeping cars – to railroads. So while rail travel could be, and usually was, an uncomfortable experience for most people in the late years of the nineteenth century, Pullman had made it possible for those who could afford it to ride in utter comfort and luxury. Cars with individual 'roomettes,' or compartments, were introduced in the 1930s.

The beginning of the end for the Pullman Company came in 1947 when an antitrust suit was brought against the company to the effect that it could no longer both manufacture and own the cars. Various arrangements were made for the Pullman cars to continue in use, but by the end of 1968 all operations came to an end.

Passenger cars of all-steel construction with massive steel underframes were in common use by the first decade

of the twentieth century. Typically, these cars had clerestory windows, and a roof that curved downward at each end of the car. While the comfort of the seats varied widely from one line to another, the passengers were much safer than they had been in wooden coaches. The last car of the 'top-of-the-line' trains was often an 'observation car' equipped with an open platform at the back. This platform was well suited for observing the countryside. It also provided a rostrum for many a politician on a whistle-stop campaign. Air conditioning, installed on some Pullman sleeping cars as early as 1929, became a fairly common amenity in the 1950s.

While the all-steel car was an important development in passenger comfort and safety, they did tend to be rather heavy. Some of the cars in use in the 1920s and 1930s weighed as much as 80 tons. This extra tonnage limited the number of cars that could be included in a train. In the 1930s, the Budd Company developed a lightweight car covered with thin stainless steel, corrugated to give it strength. Weighing in at 60 tons, these cars were light enough to be supported by four-wheel trucks. The bright stainless steel skins gave the cars the now-familiar 'modern' streamlined look characteristic of many of today's trains. With the advent of streamlining, the open-ended observation car was replaced by a picture-windowed, round-at-the-end observation car. After World War II, the dome car, providing the passenger with added vistas for sight-seeing, was introduced. These were used mainly on the scenic western routes.

Along with the stainless steel cars, another change was becoming evident in the 1940s and 1950s. More trains were being pulled by diesels and fewer by steam. While many railroad owners hailed the advent of the diesels as the harbinger of a new era of efficiency and profits, others saw them as the beginning of the end of the Golden Age.

Above: The engineer's side of the cab in the 4100 series of locomotives shows the throttle lever in the upper right. Right of the seat is the reverse lever and brake valves. The water column, upper center, is attached to the water glass and gauge cock.

Above right: From the fireman's side of the cab the firing valve and damper regulator are in the lower left, with steam gauge directly below. The large feedwater and steam heat gauges are above it. The small gauge in between shows the oil-tank air pressure. At the right is the injector starting valve and above it the extension handles to valves controlling steam to auxiliaries.

Below right: In 1937 Southern Pacific purchased the first of its modern design cab-aheads, including No 4151, in which the cab forward end was more streamlined than in earlier cab-aheads. The modern design had an overall length of 125 feet with tender and a weight of 1,028,700 pounds.

Innovations on the Rails

Diesel and electric locomotives are used on most of the world's railways today, although steam still holds out in some places, particularly in developing countries. Nowhere in the world, however, was the conversion to diesel as swift, sure, and complete as it was in North America. The move away from steam had its start in the late 1920s. The Canadian National tried a diesel locomotive in 1928. From that beginning, the conversion to diesel proceeded quickly. The last steam-powered locomotive to be ordered by a main line United States railroad was made for the Norfolk and Western Railroad in 1953. This line continued steam operation for about 10 years longer than other United States main lines, retiring its last steam locomotive in 1960.

The end of the steam era might have come much more quickly were it not for the Great Depression and World War II. However, after the war, the diesel tide overwhelmed steam:

Year	Units Ordered	
	Steam	Diesel
1944	326	750
1945	115	800
1946	86	950
1947	69	1900
1948	86	2850
1949	57	1950
1950	12	2400

Western lines, both in the United States and Canada, were among the first to embrace diesels. Before the switch to diesels, the Union Pacific had tried a locomotive powered by a 12-cylinder gasoline engine. The engine was used to pull a three-car articulated streamlined train called the

City of Salina. After a coast-to-coast tour during which it attracted a great deal of attention, the *City of Salina* went into service in 1934. However, gasoline was too volatile and expensive a fuel for the needs of railroading, a circumstance that encouraged continued interest in diesels. In the 1930s, however, diesel engines were very heavy machines with a poor weight to horsepower ratio. A breakthrough was achieved in 1933, when General Motors developed a two-stroke diesel with a ratio of 20 pounds per horsepower, a figure much improved over the typical 80 pounds per horsepower of previous diesel engines.

The Chicago, Burlington, and Quincy ordered a three-car train powered by the new General Motors engine. Called the *Pioneer Zephyr*, this streamlined train achieved an average speed of 77.5 miles an hour on its maiden run from Denver to Chicago in 1935. The Union Pacific followed with the *City of Portland* running between Chicago and Portland. This train broke speed records; a transcontinental run of 3193 miles was completed in 56 hours and 55 minutes. In trials, the train had achieved speeds of 120 miles an hour. In the same year, the Burlington inaugurated the 3000 horsepower *Denver Zephyr*. Although these trains did a great deal to publicize diesel power and 'streamliners,' the power units could not easily be used for other trains. By the mid-1930s, a number of companies had started production of straight road units which could readily be used to pull practically any train.

A number of factors contributed to the rapid dieselization of railroads in western North America. Although a number

Below: Late in 1946 Southern Pacific placed orders with Electromotive Division of General Motors for 20 diesel locomotives of 6000 horsepower each, destined to be the first of a large fleet for freight service. They were 4 (B-B) class locomotives with a cab on each end so the locomotive could be operated in either direction without being turned. The first main-line diesel freight locomotives were put into service in the following year, in 1947. Old steam locomotives had been well used during the war years and the new diesels were much more efficient on steep grades, on curves and over long distances. By 1957 Southern Pacific trains were fully dieselized. The outward appearance of the locomotives purchased remained unchanged but there were some changes in specifications. The 'B' units of locomotives purchased prior to 1949 were renumbered in the 8000s late in 1949, while the 'A' units continued to be numbered in the 6100s. Late in 1949 the first of the DEF 5 class were delivered; the 'A' units were numbered from 6240 through 6295 and the 'B' units were numbered from 8140 through 8195. Each of these latest locomotives (classed F-7 by the builders) has identical specifications: the total weight was 923,900 pounds on 16 pairs of 40-inch drivers; the starting tractive effort was 234,600 pounds; and the continuous tractive effort at 9 miles per hour (the speed at which maximum pulling efficiency is achieved) is 209,600 pounds. Each locomotive contains four 1500-horsepower 16-cylinder diesel engines of $8\frac{1}{2}$-inch bore and 10-inch stroke. The engines revolve at 800 rpm and operate direct current electric generators to power the 375-horsepower electric motors geared to each axle by a 65:12 gear ratio, giving a potential speed of 55 miles per hour. The overall length of each locomotive is 201 feet and $6\frac{1}{4}$ inches.

Opposite and below: The *City of San Francisco*, shown here at night and during the day at Oakland Pier in January 1938, was the first diesel-powered train on the Southern Pacific line and began service between San Francisco and Chicago in 1936. This train also served the Union Pacific, Chicago West and Northern Pacific lines.

of steam locomotives specially designed for use in the western mountains had been developed, these were never entirely satisfactory. The Mallets and other locomotives designed for mountain use were not economical to run in other conditions. Locomotives had to be changed before the train started on its mountain run and after it descended. Diesel units, however, proved to be versatile. Any number of units could be combined to suit the needs of any train, in any terrain. Diesels could pull trains up grades faster and around curves more surely than could any steam locomotive. Also, diesel locomotives were much simpler to operate than were steam locomotives. Engineers could be trained in less time. Of course, other economic factors were also important. At the time diesels were introduced, oil was cheaper than coal, a circumstance that had encouraged the building of oil-fired steam locomotives. Theoretically, the maintenance of steam locomotives should have been cheaper than maintaining diesels. However, over the war years,

many steam locomotives had become run down to the point where maintaining them had become disproportionately costly. Railroads found that banks were more inclined to make loans on new diesels than on old, worn-out steam locomotives.

The Union Pacific had the distinction of being the railroad that made the greatest use of gas turbines. As many as 40 of these were in active use on the Union Pacific in the late 1950s, while no other railway in the world ever went beyond the experimental use of two or three. At 8500 horsepower, these could well have been the most powerful locomotives ever built.

They were eventually discontinued in favor of the convenience of buying production diesel units from General Motors and General Electric. However, Union Pacific also used a 6200 horsepower diesel unit specially designed for use on its line. It somehow seems appropriate that this engine, one of the most powerful single-unit diesels in the

Great Northern No 3040 and three additional engines haul a long line of various box cars laden with goods between the Great Lakes and the West Coast.

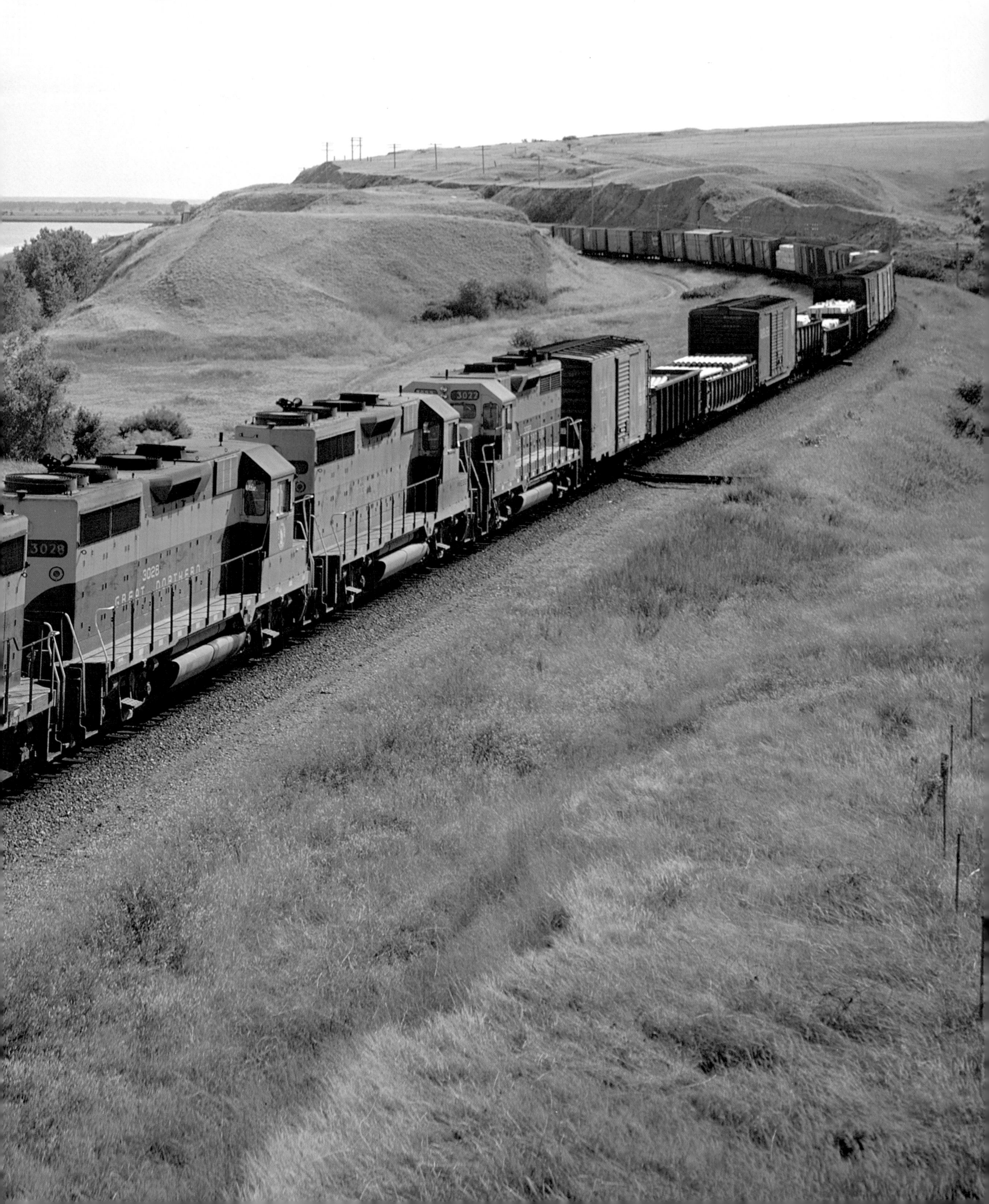
3028
3028
GREAT NORTHERN
3027

Santa Fe's *Super Chief*, the daily all-pullman streamliner between Chicago and Los Angeles, ascends the steep grades at Wooton, Colorado.

world, should be used by the line that for years provided the magnificent sight of *Big Boy* steam locomotives chuffing up a mountain grade.

By the 1950s, the takeover of western railroads by the diesel was practically complete. The Atchison, Topeka and Santa Fe was a pioneer in dieselization, obtaining its first 'growler' in 1935. The Santa Fe was given priority for getting diesels during World War II because of the vast desert expanse it ran through. Keeping water stations in the desert fully supplied had always been expensive and inconvenient. By 1943, two Santa Fe divisions were completely diesel, and full dieselization was completed shortly after the end of the war. The Denver and Rio Grande ran its last standard-gauge steam locomotive in 1952, and the Southern Pacific was all diesel by 1959. The Milwaukee Road, one of the few western railroads to try electrification, switched to straight diesel on all its lines in 1974.

The Canadian National, the first North American railway to use a diesel, was completely dieselized in 1960. However, the CN continues to operate a steam train between Toronto and Niagara Falls as a tourist attraction. The CN also maintains about 80 steam locomotives as a kind of monument to the Golden Age of Steam. The Canadian Pacific dieselized over a six-year period from 1948 to 1954. Today

Above: Southern Pacific No 3186, a modern diesel locomotive at the San Francisco yard, is used mainly for freight. The transition from steam to diesel power for locomotives took place in a short space of time in the United States and the first main-line diesel freight locomotive went into service in 1947. Diesel power was a reliable fuel source and turnaround time was faster than with steam.

Right: A wartime magazine advertisement describes the onset of diesel.

the CP operates some of the most heavily powered diesel trains in the world over its Rocky Mountain routes. Hauling 10,000 tons of block coal, these trains are powered by 11 diesel units – eight at the head and three slave units.

While practically all railways in Europe, particularly those in western Europe, are electrified, only a small percentage of North American lines are so powered. And most of the North American electrified lines are in the East rather than the West. Actually, most diesel locomotives are actually electric locomotives. The diesel engines turn dynamos which generate electricity to run motors that drive the wheels. Thus a diesel can be thought of as an electric locomotive carrying its own source of power rather than picking up power from overhead wires or a third rail, as is the case with most of the world's electric railways.

A NEW DAY DAWNS IN RAILROADING

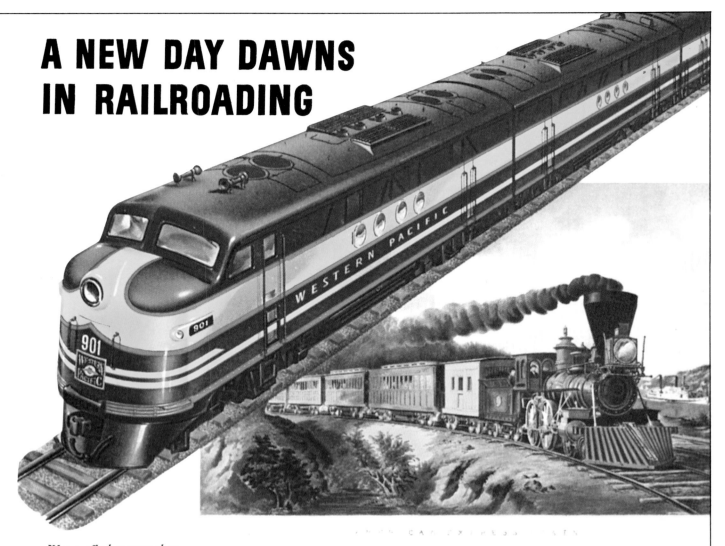

War traffic has more than doubled the volume of freight hauled by the Western Pacific Railroad from Salt Lake City to San Francisco. Wherever the going is toughest on this rugged route, General Motors Diesel freight locomotives have kept this vast stream of vital munitions moving steadily.

A crack "Express Train" of 1865 as pictured by Currier & Ives. Four years later an important new era began when the first railroad linked the Atlantic and Pacific.

Throughout history, wars have set up new milestones of transportation progress. And with this war, it is the General Motors Diesel Locomotive that is ushering in the new era. What advances the future will bring are already apparent in the present performance of these locomotives and the way they are helping to meet the abnormal demands upon the railroads today.

KEEP AMERICA STRONG · BUY MORE BONDS

War building is being rushed ahead with reliable General Motors Diesel power. In the days to come this dependable, economical power will be ready to do the hard jobs of peace.

GENERAL MOTORS

DIESEL POWER

LOCOMOTIVES......................ELECTRO-MOTIVE DIVISION, La Grange, Ill.

ENGINES..150 to 2000 H.P...CLEVELAND DIESEL ENGINE DIVISION, Cleveland, Ohio

ENGINES.....15 to 250 H.P......DETROIT DIESEL ENGINE DIVISION, Detroit, Mich.

Below: Locomotive No 6500, photographed when new, was built in 1954 for hauling passenger traffic.

Top left: Canadian National Railways was the first North American line to operate diesel engines and all its trains were dieselized by 1960. Locomotive No 1900, a switcher, was built in 1958. The engine compartment is narrower than the cab to allow improved visibility during operations.

Second from top: Another in this series of locomotives, this type of engine is used principally for freight haulage. The low nose provides good visibility from the cab.

Third from the top: CP Railroad freight locomotive 6024, painted in the red livery (new in the 1960s) and mounted on six-wheel trucks, was one of a second generation of diesel locomotives that replaced the original diesel road locomotives. Generally this engine had a higher horsepower rating than earlier diesels, from 2250 to 3000 per unit compared to the 1500 and 1600. The nose was built lower on the car and inside the cab static controls replaced old movable equipment.

Bottom left: CP Rail diesel locomotive No 4075 at Glen Yard, Montreal is a road unit of the type used for mainline passenger service. The first diesel road units were acquired in 1949, including some with 2250 horsepower engines with one axle on each three-axle truck serving as an idler, which meant that only about two thirds of the weight was available for traction. These early locomotives also had characteristically small 36-inch wheels.

A Southern Pacific freight locomotive pulls out of the tunnel at Tehachapi Loop, which was built to allow trains to gain altitude to climb the Tehachapi Mountains, north of Los Angeles. The Santa Fe locomotives are pulling out of the loop to begin the ascent. In 1983 it was announced that these two great railroad companies would be merged.

It is somewhat ironic that electrified railways have not been more successful in North America. An American, Thomas Davenport of Vermont, demonstrated electric propulsion in 1838, and government officials were expressing interest in electric traction in the 1850s. At that time, however, the electric motor could not hope to compete with steam, let alone the horse. Another American, Joseph Henry, demonstrated the principle of electromagnetic induction, the principle on which electric motors and generators are based, in the 1830s.

Even toward the beginning of the twentieth century, it seemed that the United States might be moving toward a wide adoption of electrified railroads. Another American, Frank J Sprague, provided another key invention. This was a system which allowed several powered units to be linked, so that all could be controlled from a master controller in the head car. First used on the Chicago elevated lines in 1887, the system was adopted in many parts of the world, including many American cities. It is still used today, and trains of multiple units are familiar sights on commuter lines and urban rapid transit lines.

In Europe, the concept of the electrified line was rapidly extended to main line railways. In North America, it was largely limited to city rapid transit systems and a few special situations in which steam power could not be used. New York City forbade the use of steam locomotives south of the Harlem River after 1908. An electrified, third-rail system was built to power electric locomotives that pulled trains into Grand Central Terminal. This line, run on direct current (DC), is still in operation. The first main line electric service, put in by the Baltimore and Ohio in 1905, was in a mile-long tunnel under the city of Baltimore and the Patapsco River. The New York, New Haven and Hartford electrified the track between New York and New Haven in 1907. An overhead wire, 11,000-volt alternating current (AC) 25-cycle system still in use in the early 1980s

(run by Metro-North), it shows its age with frequent breakdowns. A new 60-cycle system is scheduled to be installed later in the decade on this line, which is one of the busiest commuter rail lines in the world. In 1928, the Pennsylvania Railroad used the same system to electrify 670 of its 2200 track miles. When it was done, track along the busy Northeast corridor from Washington DC to New Haven, Connecticut was under the wires.

The only major main line electrification on a western railroad was done by the Chicago, Milwaukee, St Paul and Pacific. Started in 1914, the goal of the project was to electrify the old transcontinental route from St Paul to Seattle. By 1918, some 900 miles of the route was electrified. The concept seemed financially sound, since the power was relatively cheap water-generated electricity. Some very powerful electric locomotives were used on this line. Among them were five 'bi-polars' manufactured by General Electric. Called 'Kings of the Rails,' these locomotives utilized DC at 3000 volts. They were referred to as bi-polar because of the use of 12 slow-speed gearless motors mounted directly on the axle. They were capable of moving

Above right: A Santa Fe slug locomotive, built at Cleburne, Texas.

Right: Southern Pacific No 4806 was photographed in January 1954, after completion by Fairbanks, Morse & Company.

Below: Shown here is what was one of the world's two largest single-cab electric locomotives, both of which were once operated by the Great Northern Railway on the electrified segment of its transcontinental line in the Cascade Mountains of Washington State. The two identical locomotives were designed primarily for heavy mountain duty. Each was 101 feet long, weighed 360 tons and developed 5000 horsepower. In 1929 construction of the Cascade Tunnel in western Washington was completed, making the nearly eight-mile long railway tunnel the longest in the Western Hemisphere. Maximum elevation of the route was cut down and over 40 miles of track were replaced to make the crossing easier. Electrified lines were fully dieselized in 1956.

lines were long enough to approach the status of main line railroad. A subsidiary of Southern Pacific, at its peak in the 1920s, the line operated over 1100 miles of track. Serving more than 50 communities, lines extended some 75 miles from Los Angeles. In its heyday, more than 1500 trains a day left the main terminal in Los Angeles. The line included stretches of quadruple track, which allowed operation of fast express trains. Mountain areas were served by narrow-gauge lines on grades that exceeded seven percent.

In 1938, General Motors and Standard Oil of California bought the system and several others on the West Coast. Pacific Electric was reorganized as Pacific City Lines. They did little to disguise their intention of 'motorizing' several West Coast electric railways. The suspicion that 'motorizing' was a euphemism for the destruction of the electric railway lines was soon confirmed. In 1940, Pacific City Lines was being directly run by a consortium composed of General Motors, Firestone Rubber and Standard Oil. In that same year, they began the scrapping of several of the former Pacific Electric lines, and a local streetcar line in Los Angeles that used Pacific Electric tracks. The trains were replaced by GM buses, running on Firestone tires, powered by Standard Oil fuels. Similar events took place in and around more than 40 American large cities, including Detroit, Chicago, and New York.

In 1949, a federal jury in Chicago convicted GM of criminal conspiracy with Firestone and Standard Oil to replace electric rail transportation with buses for the purpose of monopolizing the sale of buses and related products. The conviction, however, did nothing to halt the continuing destruction of electric rail systems. GM was fined $5000, and the GM executive who played the key role in the destruction of Pacific Electric was fined one dollar.

The transportation void left by the destruction of the clean, efficient electric railways was filled by millions of smog-producing automobiles that daily jam the Los Angeles system of freeways.

a 1000-ton train up a 2.2 percent grade in the Cascade Mountains at 25 miles an hour. The system made money and resisted the diesels until 1974, when the wires were taken down and diesels replaced the electrics on the run from St Paul to Seattle.

The great western railroads such as the Santa Fe, Union Pacific, and Southern Pacific gave electrification only the briefest of looks. They were not willing to take the risk with electrification when most of the rest of the country was going diesel. If cash had to be raised in a hurry, they could always sell off some of their diesels to another line. But the demand for used electric locomotives was, at best, limited in North America, so diesel it was.

There was, however, another electrified line in the West that is worthy of mention for a number of reasons. This was the Pacific Electric which operated in and around Los Angeles from 1890 until shortly after World War II. The story of the rise and fall of this railroad is archetypical of what happened to many American railroads in the twentieth century.

The Pacific Electric was unique. It was a city streetcar line, as well as an inter-urban rapid transit line. Some of its

Evolution of the Great Northern Logo

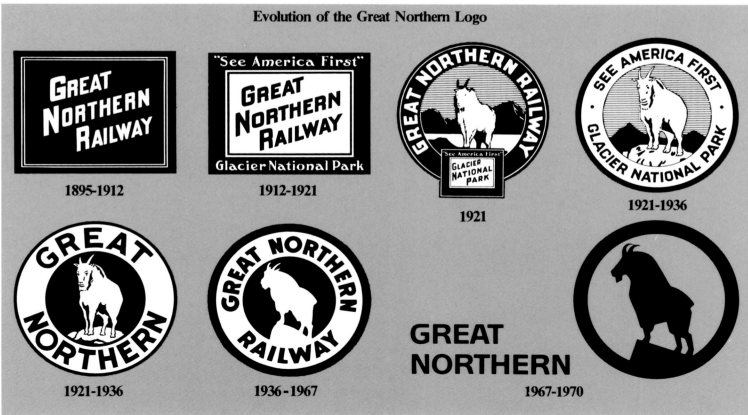

GREAT NORTHERN RAILWAY
1895-1912

"See America First" GREAT NORTHERN RAILWAY Glacier National Park
1912-1921

1921

SEE AMERICA FIRST · GLACIER NATIONAL PARK
1921-1936

1921-1936

GREAT NORTHERN RAILWAY
1936-1967

GREAT NORTHERN
1967-1970

Evolution of the Santa Fe Logo

Santa Fé Route.		Santa Fe Route	Santa Fé ·Route·	Santa Fe
1888-1895	**1895-1896**	**1896-1899**	**1899-1901**	**1901-Present**

Above left: A 1940s era diesel engine of the Great Northern stops for fuel.

Left: The St Paul & Pacific Railroad Company became the Great Northern Railway Company in 1889. 'Line' was deleted in 1894 and the first, rectangular, logo reflected the change. In 1912, when Great Northern opened hotels in Glacier National Park, the words 'See America First' were used to promote the park, with 'National Park Route' at the bottom of the rectangle. The latter was replaced in 1914 with 'Glacier National Park.' In 1921 the logo was made circular and the Rocky Mountain Goat was included because it was common in Glacier Park. From then until 1936, the wording around the logo changed, and in 1936 the profile of the goat was used.

Top: Modern freight locomotive 2649 emerges from the Santa Fe Railroad's

shop at Cleburne, Texas in 1970 after a complete rebuilding. Originally it was identical to obsolete locomotive 223, a 1945 model, which was slated for similar rejuvenation, along with several others.

Above: The logo of the Atchison, Topeka and Santa Fe Railroad Company also underwent many changes since the original design of 1888. The second logo with the lion was highly criticized and quickly changed. Several stories are told about the derivation of the one devised in 1897 and used today. Inside the tracing of a silver dollar or poker chip, a cross was drawn, symbolizing the points of the compass, a holy cross or the Indian sun god. The words 'Santa Fe,' Spanish for 'holy faith,' were placed on the cross bar and 'route' was dropped because, as a French word, it was inconsistent.

Decline and Retrenchment

As railroads prospered during the Golden Age, they were able to offer increasingly luxurious passenger service for those who could afford it. Railroads soon adopted the practice of naming their most luxurious trains. These trains, such as *The Twentieth Century Limited, The Super Chief*, and *The Coast Daylight* are to many the very essence of the lost glory of American railroading. Most of them are no more than a memory, having long succumbed to the economic realities of the decline of the railroads. However, some are still making their runs, mostly under the management of Amtrak. However, railroad enthusiasts consider these trains to be but a ghost of former glory.

The most well known of the named trains was New York Central's *Twentieth Century Limited*. One of the earliest of the luxury trains, it made its first run in 1902. By the 1920s, the New York Central was referring to it as a 'national institution,' and it was nothing less than that. Everybody who was anybody in need of traveling from New York to Chicago made the trip on the *Century*. Celebrity hounds would gather at the boarding gates in hopes of catching a glimpse of the film stars, politicians, and other notables who walked down the red carpet rolled out for the *Century* travelers.

Many *Century* travelers connected at Chicago to go on to

the West Coast in trains that vied with the *Century* for luxury and excellence of service. Luxurious, comfortable, fast trains were particularly welcome on the long runs to the West Coast, and the western lines competed fiercely for the luxury traffic.

The Atchison, Topeka and Santa Fe's *Super Chief* is as much a legend in American railroading as the *Twentieth Century Limited*. The *Super Chief* was the first diesel-powered, all Pullman streamliner in the United States. Introduced in 1937, this luxuriously appointed train made the Chicago–Los Angeles run in 39.5 hours. This time was 15 hours better than the time of its predecessor, *The Chief*. 'Extra fast, extra fine, and extra fare' was the description of *The Chief* in Santa Fe's advertising. Started in 1926, it followed two earlier luxury trains, the *California Limited* and the *Santa Fe De Luxe*. Santa Fe continued to lavish attention on the *Super Chief*, even though revenues from passenger service were little more than a tenth of earnings from freight operations.

Santa Fe did not neglect its transcontinental coach passengers. The *El Capitan* was a well-appointed all-coach train that made the Chicago–Los Angeles runs starting in 1938. The Santa Fe was particularly noted for the excellence of its food, both on the trains and in the stations. The tradition of excellence in the food service dated from 1869, when

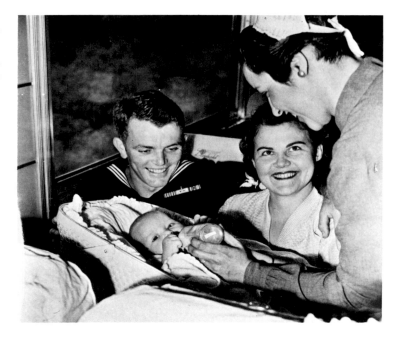

Above: Aboard the Southern Pacific *Coast Daylight* in December, 1945.

Below: The *Coast Daylight* wends its way down the coast from Oakland to Los Angeles. This train was one of the first of the passenger streamliners to be introduced in 1937.

the Santa Fe catering concession was granted to an English-man, Fred Harvey. Harvey insisted that everything, including the waitresses, had to be impeccable. The charm and respectability of the 'Harvey Girls' became a legend.

Bad times began to catch up with the Santa Fe in the late 1950s. The *El Capitan* and the *Super Chief* were combined in body but not spirit in 1960. *El Capitan* coaches and the *Super Chief* Pullmans were pulled by the same locomotive, but they were listed separately in the time tables, even though they too, of necessity, departed and arrived at the same time.

Amtrak took over Santa Fe's passenger service in 1970. However, Santa Fe insisted on a clause in the agreement to the effect that Amtrak could continue to use the names *Super Chief* and *El Capitan* only if the service continued to be proper, as judged by Santa Fe. Hardly three years later, Santa Fe felt compelled to exercise its right, and the name of Amtrak's Chicago–Los Angeles service was changed to the *South-West Limited*.

The Union Pacific's Chicago–Los Angeles service was the *City of Los Angeles*. Starting as a once-a-week, diesel-hauled, 11-car train in 1936, business was so good that a 17-car train had to be added almost immediately. By 1941, the frequency of the service had increased to every third day. After the war, the locomotives and cars were decorated in UP's golden yellow and scarlet colors. In addition to the *City of Los Angeles*, UP ran the *City of San Francisco* and the *City of Portland*, each serving the city of its name. Earlier versions of these trains were the articulated *Zephyrs*, and the *City of Salina* – the pioneer streamliner.

In addition to speed and luxury, the western railroads emphasized scenery in their advertising. Many of these routes passed through areas of spectacular scenic grandeur, and the rairlroads understandably tried to use this fact to maximum advantage. After World War II, they added cars with windowed domes that made it possible for passengers to take in much more scenery.

The *California Zephyr*, started in 1949, included five dome cars for its spectacular 2515-mile run on the tracks of the Burlington, Denver and Rio Grande, and Western Pacific Railroads. Scenery was the selling point for this train, and speed and comfort were all but ignored in the advertising. The schedule was arranged so that the train passed through the most spectacular areas in daylight. This made the trip longer, but the train was almost always solidly booked. Although the train remained popular, the lines could no longer afford to run it. By the 1970s, most of the route was taken over by Amtrak. However, the Denver and Rio Grande held on to its part of the route between Denver and Salt Lake City, calling the train the *Rio Grande Zephyr*. The Rio Grande ran the train until 1983, when they could no longer continue to absorb the losses.

Southern Pacific ran a very successful daylight service between Los Angeles and San Francisco. Appropriately called the *Daylight*, the train featured outstanding décor and fast service. When Amtrak took over the route, the name was changed to the *Coast Starlight*.

One of the more famous steam-powered trains was Denver and Rio Grande's *San Juan*. This was a narrow-gauge train that also featured scenery rather than speed. The daily service traveled the 200 miles between Durango and Alamosa, Colorado at a leisurely pace that never exceeded 35 miles per hour. When the Rio Grande ended the service in 1951, it was still powered by steam.

The Great Northern's luxury service from Chicago to the Northwest was called the *Empire Builder*. This train had a 'ranch car' that featured a coffee shop and piano-equipped lounge. The décor was western, including seats covered in pinto leather, branding irons, a western mural and rustic wood paneling and exposed beams. Started in 1929, the train was named for the founder of the Great Northern, James J Hill. Canadian by birth, he was generally called the Empire Builder.

The *North Coast Limited*, started in 1900, was a joint venture of the Great Northern and Northern Pacific and Chicago. Originally running from St Paul to Seattle, it became a Chicago to Seattle run in 1911. The Chicago,

Right: Enroute to Los Angeles from Chicago, Santa Fe Railroad's bi-level *El Capitan* climbs the grade of Raton Pass in southern Colorado, sometime before 1971.

Milwaukee, St Paul and Pacific (The Milwaukee Road) ran a series of trains called *Hiawathas*. The ultimate of these was the *Olympian Hiawatha*, a diesel-hauled luxury train from Chicago to Seattle. The *Olympian Hiawatha* was preceeded by the *North Coast Hiawatha* that ran from Chicago to St Paul–Minneapolis via Milwaukee.

Southern Pacific's prime entry in the luxury train market was the *Sunset Limited* service between Los Angeles and New Orelans. Started in 1894 as a weekly service, it was one of the first of the luxury trains. Lucius Beebe in *The Trains We Rode* said of the *Sunset Limited* '. . . the concept of a grand hotel was everywhere visible . . . in the form of watermarked stationery, silver fingerbowls, an encouraging assortment of fine whiskeys on the club cars, out-of-season strawberries, eastern lobsters and fresh brook trout on the menu. . . .' New streamlined equipment was added in 1950. By 1970, however, the *Sunset Limited* was only a shadow of what it had been, but, sadly, this was a rather typical

reflection of what had happened to American railroads. The sleepers and dining cars were gone. An automat-style buffet was the only food service available on a 44-hour run. When Amtrak took over, it restored the sleepers and diner. For a while, Amtrak operated the *Sunset Limited* as a part of a transcontinental New York–Los Angeles service with through sleepers. However, budget cutbacks in 1971 forced the removal of the through sleepers and the substitution of airline-style plastic meal trays with food out of the microwave oven for dining car service.

The ups and downs of the *Sunset Limited* are a microcosm of the problems faced by American railroads since the end of World War II. During the war, railroads in the United States and Canada performed magnificently. During World War I, the United States Government took over the railroads in the interest of wartime efficiency. The chaos that resulted convinced the authorities not to try that again. The United States remains the only major nation in

The *Empire Builder* snakes its way toward the summit of the Continental Divide near Glacier Park in 1947. The *Empire Builder* began daily service between Chicago and the Pacific Northwest in 1929. The Great Northern's fleet of top transcontinental passenger streamliners was replaced in 1947 and again in 1951, and in 1955 domes were added. The new streamliners began daily service on 23 February 1947. It took 45 hours between Chicago and Seattle or Portland. Each train consisted of 12 cars and a two-unit diesel-electric 4000-horsepower locomotive.

152

the world in which the railroads are not nationalized. However, the severe problems of American railroads over the past 30 years had resulted in greater government participation in the operation of some aspects of American railroading.

After the end of World War II, the future seemed generally bright for American railroads. However, technological advances in other transportation areas soon had the railroads in deep trouble. During the war years, no automobiles were manufactured for civilian use. Gasoline rationing precluded long trips even for those who had cars in good enough shape to make the trip. At the war's end an automobile-starved American public bought up cars as fast as they came off the assembly line. More people started to use their cars rather than the train for trips away from home. Railroads in the East began to feel the pinch of reduced revenues. For the western railroads, the automobile was not as much of a threat, particularly on the long runs of the West Coast. But the western lines had a formidable competitor – the jet airliner. When commercial air travel started to grow in the late 1930s and early 1940s, the railroads were still in a favorable competitive position. Propellor-driven aircraft of the time, such as the DC-3s, were faster than trains. But when travel time to and from airports was added, the airplane did not always come out as the best travel option. Propellor-driven airlines of the 1940s tended to be cramped, noisy and plagued with vibrations. The jet plane, however, overcame many of these limitations. They were fast and relatively quiet. The speed of the trip overcame the train's advantage of more space and wandering room. It was very difficult for a train that took some 40 hours to make the run from Chicago to Los Angeles to compete for the speed-minded passenger, when a jet plane could make the trip in 3 or 4 hours. Freight operations began to suffer too, as trucks, supplied with tax dollar-built super highways, took business away from the railroads.

Even in the halcyon days of the supertrains, it was difficult to make a profit carrying passengers. Many railroads, however, considered these trains as good advertising rather than as revenue producers, and continued to run them, subsidizing them with profits from freight operations. However, as revenues from both passenger and freight operations continued to drop, service on the super trains had to cut back. These reductions reduced their appeal, making it even more difficult to attract passengers. Highways also induced more travelers to opt for using the car on that long trip rather than taking a train.

As railroad companies began to lose astronomical amounts of money on passenger service, they abandoned the lines that were causing the biggest drains. However, abandoning lines was not a simple undertaking. Heavily regulated railroads were required by law to maintain certain passenger lines, no matter how much money was being lost. They had to petition the Interstate Commerce Commission for permission to drop them, a process that often took years.

By the 1960s, most railroads no longer concealed their desire to discontinue all passenger service if they could. The ICC ordered most to continue service, even though

trains often ran completely empty. The losses further diminished the railroad's ability to maintain equipment and track properly, a situation that was beginning to affect safety in both freight and passenger operations.

The government tried to come to the rescue with the creation of the National Railroad Passenger Corporation in 1970, operating under the name of Amtrak. Railroad companies were given the option of discontinuing long-distance passenger service in exchange for turning over their best passenger equipment to Amtrak. Most railroads

Right: The snowbound *City of San Francisco* was marooned for three days when a raging blizzard in the Sierra Nevada halted its progress in January, 1952. The train was rescued and there were no major passenger injuries.

readily accepted the Amtrak proposal and willingly divested themselves of their passenger routes. A notable exception was the Denver & Rio Grande Western, which maintained passenger service on its lines in the Rockies until 1983. There were other exceptions, such as the Southern Pacific's San Francisco Peninsula commuter service, which continued until the 1980s, but for the most part, it was the end of an era. It was also to be the beginning of an era for the railroads.

The early 1970s were a pivotal moment for all North American railroads. Shorn of the costly passenger business by the advent of Amtrak, they were able to concentrate on what they had always felt they could do best: haul freight. This was an especially important to the railroads of the West, where long distances allowed the roads to compete favorably with truck traffic. Driven to decline and cornered into retrenchment after World War II, the railroads emerged in the 1980s as viable enterprises such as they had been in their Golden Age.

They had emerged from the tunnel. The future that lay before them was not without its dangers, but for the western railroads, it was a future of promise and opportunity.

The Western Railroads Move Toward a New Century

At the beginning of the twentieth century, the railroads of the North American West were new. The first tenuous link with the East was new enough that many of those who ran the early steam on the first transcontinental railroad were still alive and some were still running steam. A railroader who was 21 when the Golden Spike was driven at Promontory was barely into his fifties when the century turned. Those who were in their 20s when Canada's transcontinental were completed, were still under 40.

Even as the rail lines were new, the network that spread out from them was extensive. The Southern Pacific and the Santa Fe had built California's infrastructure, while Jim Hill's Great Northern and Northern Pacific were doing the same for the Northwest and the northern Great Plains.

The competing efforts of the Canadian National and Canadian Pacific gave Alberta and British Columbia a choice of routes and linked the great port of Vancouver to the rest of Canada.

Throughout the twentieth century, the railroads of the West evolved and matured, and the western rail net in both the United States and Canada was gradually intermeshed with the national grid. Nevertheless, the western roads maintained their own unique character. It was a character that involved great distances and grand vistas, and hundreds of miles of single track, a feature that was common on roads like the the Santa Fe but unheard of on the great trunk routes of the East.

In mid-century there had come the collapse of the passenger business, a crisis in the freight business and the tumbling dominos of mergers and bankruptcies — but certainly more of

Below: Seven Atchison, Topeka & Santa Fe diesels lug a freight across the Tehachapis. *Opposite:* A Union Pacific local crawls through Mira Loma, California.

the latter in the East than in the West. By and large, the eastern trunk lines fared worse than the western railroads. The Chesapeake & Ohio merged with the Baltimore & Ohio, and then merged with the Seaboard which had already merged with the Atlantic Coast Line. The great Pennsylvania Railroad began the twentieth century as the self-styled 'Standard Railroad of the World,' but by the 1960s, it stumbled hard and was forced to merge with its powerful rival, the New York Central. Together these once great roads became the financially-troubled Penn Central, which tumbled into bankruptcy and oblivion before it could even repaint all its boxcars in its new livery.

In the West, Jim Hill's Great Northern and Northern Pacific merged with the Chicago Burlington & Quincy to form Burlington Northern in 1970, but they had already been sister roads for nearly a century. The biggest railroad merger story of the 1980s was that of the Santa Fe and the Southern Pacific, two of the West's legendary roads. The Atchison, Topeka & Santa Fe Railway, continuing the 1859 vision of Cyrus Holliday, operated over 11,000 miles, from Chicago to the Gulf of Mexico at Houston and Galveston, and throughout the Southwest to the West Coast ports of San Francisco, Los Angeles and San Diego.

The Southern Pacific was, meanwhile, one of the largest and busiest transportation systems in the West, dominating a swath of territory that included Oregon, California, Nevada, Colorado, Arizona and Texas. It served 15 Pacific Ocean ports, seven ports of entry into Mexico and 10 ports on the Gulf coast. Built a century before on the dreams of four men, the Southern Pacific grew from a tenuous steel track across hostile plains into one of the largest privately owned rail transportation companies in the world. Southern Pacific, which began as a golden dream to bind a continent with tracks of steel, had developed the rich resources of California and the West. In so doing, it helped bring to fruition the dreams of the millions who rode its rails to begin new lives in the West.

Southern Pacific is today the legacy of the men who tamed the Sierra, saved the Imperial Valley and united California with Texas and Oregon. Southern Pacific is the men and women who built the empire of steel so that others could build their futures in the Golden Empire.

It was on 27 September 1983 that a press release was issued jointly by Southern Pacific headquarters in San Francisco and Santa Fe headquarters in Chicago stating that the two companies had agreed in principle to `enter into a business combination.' The statement went on to say that, `Under the agreement each company would become a subsidiary of a newly-formed holding company to be called Santa Fe Southern Pacific Corporation.'

The merger of the non-rail assets of the two roads took place on 23 December 1986, with each of the railroads continuing to operate separately, each maintaining its own routes, pending the approval of the Interstate Commerce Commission (ICC). This approval was officially denied on 24 July 1986. Though Santa Fe Southern Pacific protested, the ICC emphatically stated that the merger would reduce competition in the West and told Santa Fe Southern Pacific to sell off one of the two railroads. Santa Fe Southern Pacific decided to keep the Atchison, Topeka & Santa Fe, and on 13 October 1988, the Southern Pacific merged with Rio Grande Industries, the holding company for the Denver & Rio Grande Western Railroad to form the nation's fifth largest rail network with 15,000 miles of track in 15 states, connecting the mouth of the

Below: A big EMD SD-class diesel locomotive in Southern Pacific livery photographed by DW Golde at Dolores, California.

Columbia in the Pacific Northwest to the mouth of the Mississippi on the Gulf of Mexico. The combined services of the two railroads would be marketed under the Southern Pacific Lines banner, with headquarters in San Francisco.

Dating back to 1871, the Denver & Rio Grande Western Railroad was a small but profitable road serving the central Rocky Mountain states with a hub at Denver. The Southern Pacific, meanwhile, was one of the largest and busiest transportation systems in the West. It was also a diversified 'transportation and land development' company with holdings in pipelines and telecommunications, whose vast network of steel and microwave spans what the company called `The Golden Empire,' and what others call `The Sun Belt.'

This 'empire' is an enormous marketplace of over 70 million people — representing nearly a third of the nation's population and gross national product. The gross national product of the Golden Empire exceeds that of the rest of the nation in per capita terms, and that of nearly every nation on earth in absolute terms. From this empire comes 97 percent of the nation's rice crop, 88 percent of its copper ore, 85 percent of its lettuce and grapes, 83 percent of its natural gas, 75 percent of its oil, 65 percent of its cotton and 40 percent of its lumber. It is a land of shimmering natural beauty and bountiful farms, the fastest-growing region in the country and the one with the most modern industrial base.

Meanwhile, with Southern Pacific out of the picture, the Santa Fe Southern Pacific holding company formed in 1983, changed its name to Santa Fe Pacific in April 1989.

Having been denied Southern Pacific's hand, the Atchison, Topeka & Santa Fe — through its Santa Fe Pacific parent — continued to remain open to other suitors, and after subsequent courtship, one was found. On 30 June 1994, Santa Fe Pacific announced that it would merge with North America's longest railway, the Burlington Northern — subject, of course, to the approval of the ICC. The new company was to be known as the Burlington Northern & Santa Fe Railway Company.

Under the merger plan Santa Fe shareholders would receive 0.27 shares of Burlington Northern common stock for each Santa Fe share. Burlington Northern chairman Gerald Grinstein would be chairman of Burlington Northern & Santa

Below: The would-be merger partners. A Southern Pacific freight passes a side-tracked Santa Fe train. This photograph was taken in 1987, a year after the merger was denied, but when both roads were both owned by the Santa Fe Pacific holding company. *Bottom left:* A Burlington Northern GP -class locomotive at Bend, Oregon.

Fe, while Santa Fe chairman Robert Krebs would be the president and chief executive officer. 'The combination of Burlington Northern and Santa Fe is a predominately end-to-end merger that will benefit shippers and the public,' Grinstein promised 'There is very little overlap between our two rail systems. The merged Burlington Northern/Santa Fe network will provide single-line service across the key transcontinental corridor from central and southern California to the southwestern gateways of Memphis and Birmingham. It will provide Midwestern grain shippers with new single-line access to the West Coast and Gulf ports, and will enhance shipping options to Canadian and Mexican gateways.'

It was noted that a single-line carrier would give shippers a single point of contact, and eliminate costs and delays associated with interchange of cargo between carriers. It would also blend Santa Fe's intermodal expertise with Burlington Northern's strength in coal and grain. The merger of the rails of the Atchison, Topeka & Santa Fe and the Burlington Northern held the promise of a seamless 31,000-mile mega-railroad, and a *western* mega-railroad at that. With 92,000 cars and 4400 locomotives and control of a vast network from Seattle to Los Angeles to Chicago Burlington Northern Santa Fe would be greater in scope and mileage than all the railways in most entire countries.

When the Burlington Northern Railroad was born in 1970, it was already one of North America's largest railroads. It had 24,400 miles of main line, 35 percent of which came from the Chicago, Burlington & Quincy, and 34 percent of which came from the Great Northern. There were 1990 locomotives destined for the new `Cascade Green' paint scheme, 33 percent of which came from the Chicago, Burlington & Quincy, with 31 percent coming from each of the two `Northerns.' There were 110,741 freight cars, with 66 percent equally divided between the Great Northern and the Chicago, Burlington & Quincy, and 32 percent coming from the Northern Pacific. About half of the 1284 Burlington Northern passenger cars came from the urban commuter operations of the Chicago, Burlington &

Quincy, as the other roads had retired most of their passenger cars during the 1960s.

On 21 November 1980 the St Louis-San Francisco Railway (the 'Frisco') was added to the Burlington Northern, with 431 locomotives and 17,392 freight cars operating over 4653 miles of track. The Colorado & Southern Railroad joined Burlington Northern on 31 December 1981, and the related Fort Worth & Denver was added on 31 December 1982. Together these two roads contributed 259 locomotives and 3772 freight cars operating over 1859 miles of track on a main line between Dallas-Fort Worth and Wendover, Wyoming.

By the end of its first decade, Burlington Northern operated 3200 locomotives and 109,000 freight cars—many of them acquired after 1970—over 27,000 miles of track. This compares to 24,400 miles inherited in 1970, and 30,240 miles operated in 1983.

In the first quarter century after the Cascade Green locomotives first ventured upon the tracks of the American Midwest and Northwest, the Burlington Northern Railroad serves more than 4000 American communities, including cities as large as Chicago (population three million) and hamlets as small as Bill, Wyoming (population three).

By the time of the merger announcement, the Burlington Northern had evolved into the longest rail system in North America, with 25,474 miles of track, compared to the 24,400 miles operated in 1970 and 30,240 miles at its peak in 1983. Long the longest railroad in the nation, it links Puget Sound to the Great Lakes, and reaches from Canada through vast grain, coal and timber belts in the heart of America to Gulf Coast ports in Texas, Alabama and Florida. Burlington Northern, now headquartered in Fort Worth, Texas, had 2309 locomotives (including 1227 that were leased), compared to 1990 in 1972; and 61,177 freight cars (including 14,036 that were

Below: A splendid and illustrative view of an Atchison, Topeka & Santa Fe intermodal freight train that shows the variety of cars that are used on a modern freight. The tractor-trailer rigs are an important part of Santa Fe's non-rail repertoire.

The Great Western Railroads

In 1983, the parent companies of the Atchison, Topeka & Santa Fe, and the Southern Pacific announced a merger of the two roads, which was officially rejected by the the ICC in 1986. In 1988, the Southern Pacific merged with Rio Grande Industries, the holding company for the Denver & Rio Grande Western Railroad. In 1994, the Santa Fe and the Burlington Northern announced their intention to merge. Compare this map with the one on page 62.

Burlington Northern

Denver, Rio Grande & Western

Union Pacific (incorporating Missouri Pacific)

Chicago & Northwestern

Atchison, Topeka & Santa Fe

Southern Pacific

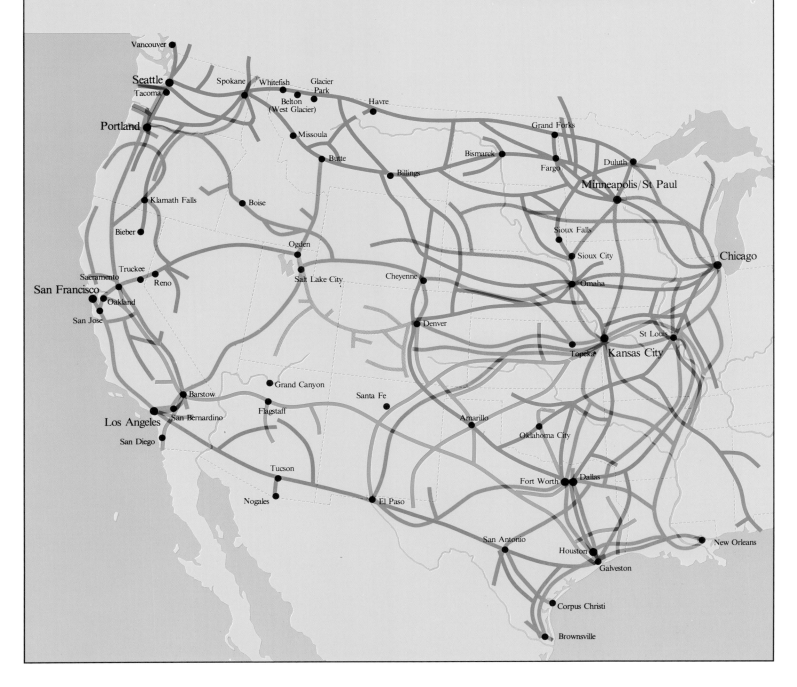

leased), compared to 100,741 in 1972 at the time of the merger. Of the freight cars, 41 percent were covered hoppers (used primarily for Burlington Northern's coal operations), 26 percent were gondolas and open-top hoppers, and 17 percent were boxcars. There were 601 cabooses and 141 commuter passenger cars in service. The latter figure compares to the 1284 commuter cars with which Burlington Northern started in 1972.More than 32,000 railroaders keep the Burlington Northern working across America—moving its coal, grain, lumber, manufactured products and countless other goods. Of the 25,474 miles of track, 16,078 miles were main line, 6433 miles were branch lines owned by the company, while 2963 miles were operated under trackage rights. At the end of 1989, approximately 18,954 miles of the railroad's tracks consisted of 112-pound per yard (or heavier) rail, including approximately 9059 track miles of 132-pound per yard or heavier rail. At that same date, 8365 miles of track were equipped with centralized traffic control signaling systems and there were 14,002 track miles of continuous welded rail in place. In the 1980s and 1990s the transportation of coal was the railroad's largest source of revenues, contributing a 32.65 percent share in 1989. Approximately 91 percent of the railroad's 1989 coal traffic originated in the Powder River Basin of Montana and Wyoming, and was primarily destined for coal-fired electric generating stations in the North Central, South Central, Mountain and Pacific regions of the United States. The balance of the railroad's coal traffic came from mines in the Midwest and the South.

Nearly all coal tonnage transported by the railroad was carried in unit trains, typically consisting of 108 hopper or gondola cars, each with a capacity of 102 tons, powered by three to six locomotives.

Meanwhile, Burlington Northern had continued to expand the use of double-stack cars in its intermodal service, offering better economies than standard flatcars. BN America, the company's domestic containerization program, began utilizing the double- stack technology in selected traffic lanes in the early 1990s.

Union Pacific, the railroad chartered in 1862 to build a line from Omaha, Nebraska to the Pacific, is still headquartered in Omaha, and it is still one of the West's great railroads. Its dis-

Below: While the Electromotive Division (EMD) F-class locomotives were originally put on the lines in the 1940s and were generally withdrawn by the 1970s, Burlington Northern kept them in service on rons between St Paul and Chicago until well into the 1980s. This one was photographed in 1984 at Aurora, Illinois. *Below left:* A Union Pacific SD-class locomotive in the Colton yards.

tinctive golden livery — reflecting the gold of the Golden Spike — is a common site from the plains and mountains of Colorado, to the Oregon side of the Columbia Gorge, to the sagebrush-studded hills of southern California where you can smell the salt air of the Pacific.

Today an important part of the Union Pacific portfolio is the 11,547-mile Missouri Pacific (MoPac) Railroad that also now wears the Union Pacific gold livery. In the 1970s, the MoPac system took over the Chicago-based Chicago & Eastern Illinois Railroad and later the Texas & Pacific Railway. In 1980, stockholders voted to approve a merger of the Missouri Pacific and the Union Pacific lines.

Another member of the Union Pacific portfolio is the 2175-mile Missouri-Kansas-Texas Railroad, the KT line, or simply the 'Katy.' Originally a line between New Orleans and Northern Kansas, the Katy today operates primarily between the Gulf Coast at Galveston and Omaha/Council Bluffs. Union Pacific executives have long considered the Katy a vital part of the Union Pacific's main route between Kansas and Texas because of trackage rights agreements. Because the sound welfare of the Katy has always been of vital importance to the Union Pacific, the Union Pacific merged with the Katy in 1988, when the smaller line was beset with severe financial difficulties.

In 1989, joined with members of the management team of the Chicago & NorthWestern Railroad to form a limited partnership to buy the road and Union Pacific now owns a quarter of the Chicago & NorthWestern Railroad.

The Union Pacific in turn divested itself of its petroleum and real estate activities in 1988 and 1989 in order to concentrate on its core business — railroading. The realization of the nation's dream to span the continent, the Union Pacific today is the third largest railroad system in the United States. Its 24,000 miles of track serve 22 states, with main lines extending from Chicago in the midwest to Los Angeles, Oakland and Seattle in the west and El Paso, Houston and New Orleans in the south.

In Canada, the two major roads are neither eastern nor western railroads, but national railroads. Nevertheless, both the Canadian National and the Canadian Pacific play important roles in western Canada, not the least of which is to unite Alberta, British Columbia and the Prairie provinces to the rest of the nation.

Below: A pair of Union Pacific road switchers pull a freight through City of Industry, California. *Below left:* A Union Pacific SD-class locomotive.

Both companies regularly touch the day-to-day lives of western Canadians. In addition to the movement of people and products by rail, they operate trucking lines and extensive telecommunications networks.Most of the track built before the 1920s ran across Canada from east to west to bind the nation together. Over the recent decades, Canadian National has been building lines to the north, to transport ore from areas where minerals have been discovered. Hauling many tons of raw materials over long distances is a job railways do best, and most of the new lines do it very well. The longest one, the Great Slave Railway, stretches from northern Alberta into the Northwest Territories.

While Canadian National is a diversified company with activities ranging from real estate to telecommunications, the rail business still accounts for 90 percent of Canadian National's portfolio. These traditionally included the Canadian National Railway as well as the separate subsidiary railways active in 13 of the United States operated by Canadian National's Grand Trunk Corporation. On 1 January 1992, Canadian National merged its railway activities in Canada with those of the Grand Trunk Corporation, which comprised three regional rail systems: the Grand Trunk Western Railroad, the Central Vermont Railway, and the Duluth, Winnipeg & Pacific Railway, which together served the northeastern and midwestern United States.

Operating functions previously managed independently on either side of the border were integrated to permit joint planning and better service coordination. Canadian National Marketing's commodity-based business units were now under single management, creating unified focus and capability in the Canadian and United States marketplace. The result of this move is an entity known as CN North America. It serves as an umbrella for all of Canadian National's railway operations.

CN North America accounts for more than 90 percent of the corporation's business activity, two-thirds of which involve the movement of international traffic — by intermodal service between Canada, offshore and the United States, and of bulk commodities handled for export.

In 1992, Canadian National acquired 25 new fuel efficient locomotives from GE Locomotives Canada and 400 intermodal containers and chassis. Monon Corporation of Indiana

Below: A Canadian National (now CN North America) freight. In 1992, Canadian National consolidated all of its rail activities under the CN North America banner. *Below left:* A Canadian National F-class cowl unit.

built the chassis and 250 of the containers, while Canadian National's own TransTech facility in Moncton produced 150 containers. Canadian National also bought 347 new and rebuilt auto carriers from National Steel Car of Hamilton, Ontario, to handle increased automobile traffic.

In 1993, Canadian National acquired 500 100-ton capacity boxcars for wood pulp, 250 insulated containers and 190 chassis, and 54 bi-level automobile carriers. It will increase the capacity to 700 boxcars for handling aluminum ingots and wood pulp, and modify 104 covered hopper cars for watertight cement shipments.

Major plant improvements paved the way for continent spanning double stack container service in 1992. These included track clearances to accommodate higher trains, especially in the mountainous areas of Western Canada.

At the close of the twentieth century, Canadian National moved almost three times as much freight as it did in the middle of the century, using 43,000 fewer freight cars and about half the locomotives.

As part of its western railroad operations, Canadian Pacific Rail has one of the longest tunnels in North America — the Connaught Tunnel in British Columbia is five miles, 117 feet long — and operates over the longest and highest bridge in Canada: the Lethbridge Viaduct in Alberta is 5328 feet long and 314 feet high.

In 1983, Canadian Pacific Rail began work on its $600 million Rogers Pass Project, the largest such undertaking since the completion of the transcontinental tracks in the 1880s. The project includes double tracking and the construction of a nine-mile tunnel through the Selkirk Mountains in British Columbia. The project will reduce the approach grade for westbound trains from the current 2.2 percent on the steepest parts of the line. When completed a decade later, the tunnel became the largest in North America.

For the last three decades of the twentieth century and into the twenty-first, passenger service in the United States and Canada has been operated by the national governments of the two countries. In 1970, the United States Congress formed the National Rail Passenger Corporation. Known simply as Amtrak, the National Rail Passenger Corporation began in 1971 to take over the passenger routes abandoned by the major railroad companies.

Below: An Alco C-class road switcher in Canadian Pacific livery.
Below left: A Canadian Pacific M-class road switcher in the yard. Canadian Pacific is Canada's second largest railway company.

Below: A pair of EMD F40PH locomotives pulling Amtrak's *Desert Wind*. The F40PH is a 3000hp diesel designed to haul double-decker passenger cars on Amtrak's western lines. *Below:* A VIA Rail Canada F40PH in Vancouver.

In the West, Amtrak operates a portfolio of routes based on the great routes of the classic era. As in the classic era, the golden age of American rail travel that existed in the first half of the twentieth century, the hub for westward-bound passengers is still Chicago. From Chicago, one has a choice of the *Empire Builder*, which follows the route of the classic Great Northern streamliner of the same name to Seattle; the *California Zephyr*, which follows the well-travelled historic route of the original transcontinental to San Francisco; and finally the *Southwest Chief*, which follows the route of the old Santa Fe *Super Chief* and *Chief* to Los Angeles.

At Salt Lake City, passengers on the *California Zephyr* may turn north to Portland on the *Pioneer*, or south to Los Angeles on the *Desert Wind*. Having reached the Pacific Coast, an Amtrak passenger may travel between Los Angeles and Seattle via San Francisco and Portland on the *Coast Starlight* which is configured to evoke the memory of the Southern Pacific's *Daylights* and *Starlights*. The Southern Pacific's classic *Sunset Route* between Los Angeles and New Orleans is now served by Amtrak's *Sunset Limited*.

Today, passenger trains in Canada are operated by the crown corporation VIA Rail Canada, headquartered in Montreal. VIA was created by the Canadian government in 1977 as a passenger subsidiary of Canadian National and today it manages all former passenger rail service in Canada except for commuter trains. Canadian National's and Canadian Pacific's passenger equipment was in turn taken over in March and September 1978, respectively. During this reorganization, combinations and discontinuations of trains occurred. Canadian Pacific sold VIA more than 300 passenger rail cars to get the government service rolling. Although VIA owns no track, it operates over the tracks of other railroads and employs more than 4000 workers. Meanwhile, locomotive engineers, brakemen and conductors remain on the payrolls of either the Canadian Pacific or the Canadian National.

In September 1978 the two major transcontinental trains in Canada, Canadian National's *Super Continental* and Canadian Pacific's *Canadian*, were combined east of Winnipeg. A notable discontinuation occurred when Canadian National's *Montreal-Halifax Scotian* was replaced by an extension of Canadian Pacific's *Montreal-St Johns Atlantic Limited* to Halifax. Although the *Atlantic's* route through northern Maine

provided a faster route than the earlier Canadian Pacific one, it was nevertheless discontinued in 1981. VIA now travels over more than 14,000 miles of track with regular passenger service.

In 1981 and 1982, VIA took delivery of the first group of Canadian-built LRC (Light, Rapid, Comfortable) locomotives and cars. LRC locomotives and cars, equipped with automatic attitude-tilt mechanisms, are designed for operation at speeds up to 125 mph.

In the early 1990s, VIA began operating its Silver & Blue class aboard the restored Western Transcontinental train, the *Canadian*. Silver & Blue class includes private quarters, a sleeping car with shower facility, and exclusive use of the Park Car with its famous dome and lounges. The *Canadian's* run is a full 3-day trip between Toronto and Vancouver.

As the twentieth century draws to a close, the railroads of the North American West have matured. The powerful lines cut at great travail through rugged mountains and parched desert by men born in Ireland and Pennsylvania and in China and California still hum with life. The first tenuous link with the East via Promontory was abandoned in 1942, and the rails were torn up two decades before the centennial of the Golden Spike, but today the yellow, blue, green, red and black freight cars of the western railroads still thunder across the nearby plains by the thousands.

The men who ran the early steam on the early transcontinental railroads are long gone but their grandsons — and yes, their granddaughters — are still running the big G-class diesels painted in the colors of railroad companies that they would still recognize.

The vast network of rail lines that have spread out from the original western railroads to serve cities and towns like Revelstoke and Whitefish and Flagstaff and Klamath Falls are still there, and the steel is polished to a gleaming finish through constant use.

Above: An EMD GP40 in Southern Pacific livery. The GP40 is a powerful 3000hp road-switcher developed for high-density operations such as Southern Pacific has in the far west. *Left:* An EMD SD45 with its distinctive long radiator leads the way as a Santa Fe freight snakes through Blue Cut on California's Cajon Pass.

A Western Rail Portfolio

A westbound Great Northern freight train hugs the Little Spokane River west of Milan, Washington in 1966.

Left: An old steam train cuts through the rugged Colorado mountains in spring. *Above:* A Cosubres & Toltec narrow-gauge train bursts through fall foliage.
Top: A Denver & Rio Grande Western steam engine chuffs across the stark,
     snow-covered flat land three miles west of Chama, New Mexico in 1968.

Denver, Rio Grande & Western engines 478 and 476 pull out of Alamosa, Colorado in full steam.

Left: A steam locomotive loaded with goods leaves Emkay, Wyoming in 1958.

Top: Tank cars load up at the C&H sugar plant in Crocket, California.

Above: This motorized utility car replaced the old-fashioned hand trucks on the Southern Pacific railway line.

Next page: Modern Canadian National diesel engines in Tascherean Yard, Montreal.

Above left: A steam locomotive hauls two passenger cars through the Colorado hills near Georgetown.

Above: A Canadian National diesel train pulls into the station at Jasper.

Below: SP diesel locomotive 2536 at rest in the San Francisco yard.

Next page: Union Pacific 4022 Big Boy engine hauls a heavy load across Wyoming, west of Speer, in July 1957.

Equipped with No 5 SA
Worthington Feedwater
Heater.

Class GS-3, GS-80 26/32 267/B-109 - SF
Boiler Pressure 280 lbs.

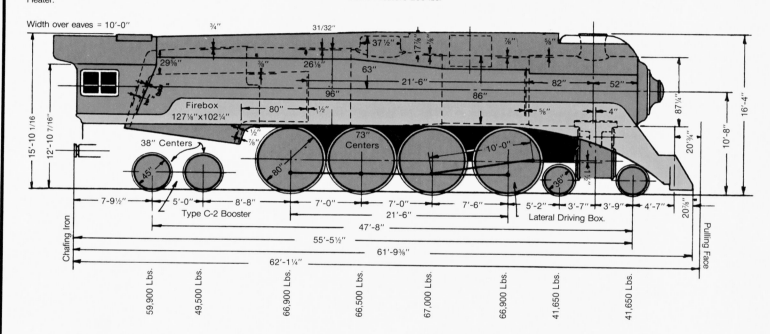

Specifications for the GS-2 and GS-3 Steam Locomotive Classes

	GS-2	GS-3			GS-2	GS-3
Weight in Working Order, Pounds			**Boiler**			
On drivers	275,700	267,300	Diameter		OD front 86″	OD front 96″
Engine truck	81,300	83,300	Pressure		300 lbs	280 lbs
Trailer truck	118,000	109,400				
Total engine	475,000	460,000	**Cylinders**			
Tender 2/3 capacity loaded	313,730		Diameter		$25\frac{1}{2}″$	26″
			Stroke		32″	32″
Tractive effort			Diameter driving wheels		80″	80″
Main cylinders	64,760	62,800				
With booster	79,660	76,650	**Wheel base**			
			Driving		21′ 6″	21′ 6″
			Engine		47′ 8″	47′ 8″
			Engine and tender		96′ 3″	96′ 3″

Class GS-3

Driving axle journals-main	13″ × 14″	Length of boiler tubes	21′ 6″	Heating surface-evaporating	4890 sq ft
Driving axle journals-front	12″ × 14″	Number of boiler tubes	49′ $2\frac{1}{4}$″ and	Heating surface of super-	
Driving axle journals-others	12″ × 14″		198′ $3\frac{1}{2}$″	heater	2565 sq ft
Engine truck journals	$7\frac{1}{2}″ × 14″$	Heating surface of boiler		Heating surface-combined	7455 sq ft
		tubes	4502 sq ft	Boiler capacity	102.3 %
Trailing truck journals	front 7″ × 14″,	Heating surface of firebox	388 sq ft	Tractive effort to adhesive wt	.235
	back 9″ × 14″				

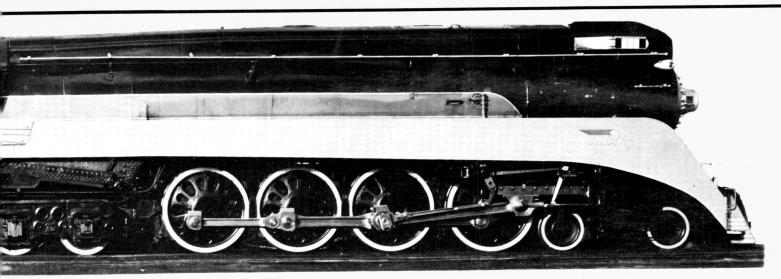

Above: One of the 20 new Southern Pacific 4-8-4 locomotives, in red, orange, black and silver livery, ordered from the Lima Locomotive Works ready for service (see pp 146–7). Early in 1937 Southern Pacific placed in service its first streamlined GS (General Service) locomotives, numbered 4410 through 4415, the GS-2s. These mighty engines were designed especially to power the luxury trains, including the *Daylight*s on the coast run because they needed high speed for fast schedules, sufficient tractive effort for the 2.2-percent grade near Santa Margarita and flexibility to negotiate curves up to 100 degrees. Engine 4411 developed 4500 horsepower at 55 mph and had a top speed of 90 mph, although 75 mph was the highest operating speed allowed. Later that same year,

Southern Pacific acquired its GS-3 locomotives numbers 4415 to 4429, which were exactly the same as the GS-2 in appearance. However, the boiler pressure was stepped up to 280 pounds and nickel steel was used in making the boiler. Tractive effort delivered to the drivers was 62,800 pounds and another 12,300 pounds was developed by the booster engine. The GS-4 locomotives were placed in service in 1941 and were the last in this series of a great breed of engines before being eclipsed by the age of diesel. The GS-4s were assigned to haul freight after World War II.

Below: The boiler inside the engine of the GS-2 locomotive.

Index

Yardman Cecil Lince at Southern Pacific's San Francisco terminal sees out the age of steam in early 1947.